D0641197

# METAPHYSICS AND ESSENCE

# METAPHYSICS AND ESSENCE

MICHAEL A. SLOTE

New York
NEW YORK UNIVERSITY PRESS

ISBN 0-8147-7761-9

Library of Congress Card Number LC-7425322

Metaphysics and Essence *is published in the United
Kingdom and Commonwealth by Basil Blackwell in
the Library of Philosophy and Logic series under the
editorial supervision of P. T. Geach, J. L. Mackie,
P. F. Strawson, David Wiggins and Peter Winch.*

Printed in Great Britain

To my father and mother

# Contents

# Preface

This book has been a long time in the making, and there are many people I would like to thank for helpful comments and criticisms. Among them are: D. Benfield, G. Boolos, J. Cugini, J. Forrester, L. Goble, D. Levin, H. Levin, R. Nozick, A. Plantinga, S. Shoemaker, R. Shope, and M. D. Wilson. I am particularly indebted to Gilbert Harman and Peter Unger, whose suggestions helped this book to assume its present form. Most of all I would like to thank Saul Kripke, whose ground-breaking logical and philosophical work and acute criticisms of the present book I have enormously profited from, and Sidney Morgenbesser, who shepherded this book to its present condition with many helpful criticisms and much encouragement.

I would also like to thank the Columbia University Council for Research in the Humanities and the Research Foundation of the State University of New York for grants that enabled me to work on this book. And I am grateful to Toni Vogel Carey for preparing the index, and to the editors of this series for their suggestions.

# Introduction

This book is an attempt at analytic metaphysics whose major tools are the concepts of essence and accident. These notions have antecedents in Aristotle[1] and have frequently been used in the philosophical literature of recent times. Roughly speaking, in our terminology, a property $p$ is essential to an entity $e$ if and only if $e$ (logically or metaphysically)[2] could not have failed to have $p$. A property $p$ is accidental to an entity $e$ if and only if $e$ has $p$, but (logically or metaphysically) could have failed to have $p$.[3]

Essentialism, which is, roughly, the view that various entities have certain of their properties essentially, has long been in eclipse, if not in disrepute. Quite recently, however, many philosophers have taken interest in Essentialism and have attempted to defend particular essentialistic claims. I shall examine various such claims here, but that will not be the major concern of this book. Rather, I shall be chiefly attempting to make use of the notions of essence and accident, and the *de re* modal notions in terms of which those notions are definable, in a way that, as far as I can tell, they have never previously been used.

[1] See *Topics*, Book I, Ch. 5, for example.
[2] I shall not distinguish logical impossibility from metaphysical impossibility.
[3] In many or even most cases, an object can have properties essentially without having the property of existence essentially, without being a necessary existent.

Consider, for example, the (putative) distinction between processes and events like soil-erosion and baseball games, on the one hand, and 'things' like tables, flowers, and lakes, on the other. Many philosophers of highly different persuasions on other matters—e.g., Heraclitus, Engels, Russell, Broad, and Goodman—have felt that the constantly changing objects we meet with in the world *are* processes (or events) or else are not significantly *different* from processes (or events). Other philosophers have felt that there clearly *is* some important philosophical distinction to be made between processes and events, and such things as tables, flowers and lakes, but have found it difficult to state just what this distinction is, or thus to justify the claim that tables, etc., are not processes or events. What I hope to show here is that the sorts of entities we call events or processes are essentially different from those we think of as 'things' that are *not* processes or events. I shall claim that such entities as baseball games and soil-erosion have essential to them properties that are not essential, say, to tables or lakes. From this conclusion will come a surprising result, namely, that the notions of process and event can be defined in terms of the notion of essence, in terms of the notion of an entity's being essentially thus and so, or having a certain property essentially. For if (speaking loosely and roughly) it is necessary that all and only processes have a certain, possibly complex property $x$ essential to them, but not necessary that all and only processes have $x$ *simpliciter*,[4] then one can define '(is a) process' as '(is an) entity with $x$ essential to it'. And similarly with the concept of an event.

I shall call any definition that defines a general metaphysically important concept largely by using some combination of claims about what is essential or what is (at most) accidental[5] to entities falling under that concept, a *definition by essence and*

---

[4] This further assumption is important, since if it is true, then we cannot avoid using the notion of essence in our definition of processhood simply by defining '(is a) process' as '(is an) entity possessing $x$'.

[5] $p$ is at most accidental to $e$ if and only if $e$ lacks $p$ or has $p$ accidentally.

*accident.*[6] I shall attempt to show that such definition by essence and accident is possible and advisable not only with respect to the notions of process and event, but also with respect to a large number of other important notions, notions like 'change', 'alteration', 'motion', 'future', 'past', '(conscious or animate) being' or 'self', 'physical', and 'physical body'. These definitions, furthermore, will require only a very limited number of primitive (undefined) concepts or concept-clusters. The notions to be used as primitives in our definitions will in many ways come close to those used by Plato, Aristotle, Hume, and Kant as central or fundamental to their philosophies. But previous philosophers, however similar their central or fundamental concepts were to those I shall be using here, however much they used the notions of essence and accident, and whatever definitions they attempted, did not use the concepts of essence and accident (or the *de re* modal concepts in terms of which they can be defined) as the key to defining some of our most basic general concepts or categories, in the way that I shall be doing here. Moreover, even if the particular definitions by essence and accident that I shall propose are mistaken, the *technique* of definition by essence and accident is, I think, important in and of itself, inasmuch as it offers new possibilities to those working in metaphysics and, perhaps, in other areas of philosophy.

In attempting to produce definitions of key metaphysical notions, it will also be necessary to use modal notions *de re* in order to clarify a number of questions about the nature and interrelations of various kinds of entities, both abstract and concrete. In order to define what it is to be an (animate) being by essence and accident, for example, I shall have to distinguish what is essential or (at most) accidental to beings from what is essential or (at most) accidental to such closely related but (putatively) abstract entities as species or races of beings; pairs, trios, etc., of beings; social groups and institutions; states of

[6] A definition by essence and accident need not explicitly contain those two notions as long as it makes use of those modal notions *de re* in terms of which one can define the notions of essence and accident.

affairs involving beings; and facts about beings. To this end, I shall put forward and (somewhat later) defend certain general theories about the existence conditions and identity conditions of species, pairs, facts, states of affairs, groups, and institutions. Our definitions by essence and accident and our discussions of various sorts of entities, however, will not, by and large, assume either that there are or that there are not such entities as facts, states of affairs, species, propositions, or properties. Conceptual analysis or clarification of what is involved in the existence of one or another (kind of) abstract or concrete entity typically need not make any commitment, one way or the other, about the existence of such entities. And this is all to the good, I believe, since there seem to be no really convincing arguments around to prove either the existence or the non-existence of (abstract) entities like facts, species, etc. Furthermore, our attempts to clarify what certain kinds of abstract entities are like *if* they exist will, I hope, have the effect of making such entities seem less mysterious and thus making it more plausible to think that such entities really do exist; and this should at least justify our using definitions whose validity does not depend on the truth of some form of Nominalism.

Before proceeding to our main task of metaphysical definition, let us first look briefly at certain important recent developments in Essentialism.

# 1. The Interest of Essentialism

Understood platonistically, Essentialism holds, at the very least, that some things have some of their properties essentially. An Essentialist who wishes to avoid commitment to properties can say that for some singular term $a$ and some predicate expression $f$, ⌜there is an $x$ identical with $a$ such that $x$ logically cannot fail to (be) $f$⌝ is or would be true.[1] Many philosophers— e.g. Quine—have denied the legitimacy or meaningfulness of Essentialism. Sometimes they simply object to the use of logical necessity or possibility in general; often they claim that the quantification into modal contexts (*de re* modality) that Essentialism involves is impermissible. There have also, however, been many attempts to answer these objections, some of them, I think, quite forceful and convincing.[2] And so I shall not here defend the meaningfulness or legitimacy of essentialistic language.[3]

[1] Those unfamiliar with 'corners' can treat them as quotation marks or see Quine's discussion of them in *Mathematical Logic*, N.Y.: Norton, 1940, sect. 6.

[2] See, e.g., R. Cartwright, 'Some Remarks on Essentialism', *J. Phil.* 65, 1968, pp. 615–26; S. Kripke, 'Naming and Necessity' in Davidson and Harman, eds., *Semantics of Natural Language*, Dordrecht: 1972; A. Plantinga, *The Nature of Necessity*, Oxford: 1974.

[3] Except to rebut one prevalent, important argument against the legitimacy of essentialistic language. In 'Quantifying In' (*Synthèse* 19, 1968, p. 181), D. Kaplan claims that the existence in ordinary talk of (implicit) quantification into belief contexts give us reason to think such quantification makes sense, whereas the absence of talk involving *de re* necessity, in ordinary language, is an argument against the legitimacy of *de re* (alethic) modality. But just as we in ordinary speech distinguish the

Many philosophers criticize Essentialism on the grounds not of its unintelligibility, but of the triviality or uninterestingness of those essentialistic claims that can be known to be true. Some philosophers, for example, have been inclined to hold that it is impossible to identify entities across possible worlds, and thus that every (contingent) entity exists in at most one possible world.[4] On one natural interpretation, it follows from all this that all of any given (contingent) entity's properties—at least aside from certain properties that involve its relation(s) to actuality or what is actual—are essential to it. And this consequence would, I think, deprive Essentialism of much of its interest. There have, however, been forceful replies to the views just described;[5] and I shall assume that transworld identification of entities and individuals is possible.

One reason, I think, why many philosophers and logicians find it hard to understand how an individual can exist in more than one possible world is the very usage of the term 'possible world' in modal logic and philosophy. Any time one considers a possible world and then attempts to imagine certain differences in it, other than certain differences in its relation(s) to what is actual,[6] one is imagining a different possible world, one not identical with the one first considered. Given this narrow way of individuating worlds, it is natural for philosophers and modal logicians to individuate entities within those worlds in the same

de dicto 'I believe that someone is a spy' from the de re 'there is someone I believe to be a spy', we can distinguish the de dicto 'I cannot avoid meeting someone today' from the perfectly ordinary, but de re 'there is someone I cannot avoid meeting today'. De re alethic modality in fact abounds in common parlance.

[4] See Chisholm, 'Identity Through Possible Worlds: some Questions', Noûs I, 1967, pp. 1–8; D. Lewis, 'Counterpart Theory and Quantified Modal Logic', J. Phil. 65, 1968, pp. 113–26.

[5] See Kripke, op. cit.; Plantinga, op. cit.; and R. Purtill, 'About Identi ty Through Possible Worlds', Noûs II, 1968, pp. 87–9.

[6] Such properties as actually existing or being actually thought about are such that whether one imagines a possible world to have them or lack them need make no difference to which possible world one is imagining. I was reminded of this by Alvin Plantinga.

narrow way and hold that every entity existing in some possible world exists in just that world and essentially has a history exactly like the history it has there. 'Possible worlds' terminology is misleading, because it goes against ordinary usage of the term 'world'. Ordinarily when we speak of things possibly having been different in some appropriate way from the way they in fact are and have been, we say that the world would have had a different history if those imagined circumstances had obtained, but do not say that in those different circumstances another world would have existed. Indeed, possible worlds, as spoken of in technical discourse, are individuated in the same way that possible histories of the world, as ordinarily conceived, are individuated, so I think that the possible *worlds* of modal logicians and philosophers really just *are* possible *histories* of the world, as ordinarily conceived. Once we realize that this is so, it should become easier for us to think of particular individuals as existing in more than one world; for if there are different possible histories of *the world*, why should there not be different possible histories of a particular *individual* in such a world? But different histories of an individual imply different total histories of the world, so if individuals could have had different histories, they could have existed in different possible histories of the world, and thus in different worlds, given technical usage of 'world'.

However, even if Essentialism cannot be shown to be uninteresting because almost all properties are essential to the entities that have them, it might still be wondered whether there are any interesting non-trivial cases of essential properties. When asked for examples of essential properties, essentialists often say, e.g., that any given person is essentially self-identical and essentially not the number five or that the man Cicero is essentially identical with Cicero (or with Tully). But these seem to many people not to be terribly interesting claims, and if Essentialism cannot do better, perhaps Essentialism is of little philosophical importance.

Quite recently, however, some rather interesting and non-trivial suggestions have been made about the essential properties of individuals. Kripke has suggested that if a given table was originally made of wood, then that table is essentially originally made of wood—even if it could *later* turn to gold or silver.[7] And in *The Problem of Knowledge*, A. J. Ayer suggests that Philomela (a woman of mythology) could not conceivably have originated as a nightingale, even though she can and does turn into one.[8] These views about essence, if true, would be of some interest. But strong doubts can, I think, be raised about their truth. With regard to Kripke's claim about the essential origins of tables, for example, consider the following putative counterexample. Imagine that a given table *t* that is in fact always wooden came from a particular block or hunk of wood *w*. What if *w*—perhaps via certain changes and rearrangements of its subatomic particles—had been steadily and lawfully changing from wood to silver and back again before the table was in fact made? Could we not imagine *t* being made out of *w* while *w* was in its silver stage instead of being made out of *w* before *w* ever changed to silver? In other words, would it not be possible for table *t* to have been made from something silver, and have been silver itself originally, and then perhaps later have turned to wood? If so, then such things as tables are at least in some cases only accidentally composed of that substance, e.g. wood, of which they are in fact originally composed. If we assume that a table can change from wood to silver, then perhaps an originally wooden table can be only accidentally originally wooden, and there is genuine doubt about Kripke's interesting essentialistic claim. And similar doubt could, I think, be generated in a similar manner about Ayer's claim that Philomela is essentially originally human.

Note that in the above supposed counterexample case where *t* is originally silver, we still imagined *t* to come or originate from the particular block *w*. That is because it seems plausible to hold

[7] *Op. cit.*, and also in 'Identity and Necessity' in M. Munitz, ed., *Identity and Individuation*, N.Y.: 1971.

[8] Harmondsworth: Penguin, 1956, p. 183.

that if a certain table was made from a given block of wood, then that very table could not have been made from any other discrete, coeval, similar block of wood. It is also plausible to think that if a given table derives from certain particular matter, it essentially derives from that matter, or at least could not possibly have come from any other matter. For similar reasons one could claim that if a person derives from a particular sperm and egg or from certain matter, he essentially derives from them, or at least could not have originated from completely different things or matter. Such views have been amply defended by Kripke,[9] and I shall not undertake any further defence of them here. But even if such claims are extremely plausible, it might be claimed that in general facts about which particular entities various other entities could or could not have emerged from are not very interesting, philosophically, so we have perhaps still not found any clear-cut and interesting examples of essential properties, or at least of essential properties that critics of Essentialism would have to find interesting or important.[10]

Of course, it might be pointed out that even within the realm of contingent entities,[11] there are different ontological categories of things and that members of different categories are essentially different, are possessed of different properties essentially. I, for example, am perhaps essentially an (animate) being or a self, whereas physical objects like tables clearly are not. But the opponent of Essentialism could grant such claims but find them uninteresting. After all, he might say, we already knew that there were ontological categories of entities and that things

---

[9] *Operibus citatis.*

[10] I am not trying to argue against anti-essentialist claims of uninterestingness, even where such argument is possible. In any case, the essentialistic claims we have not criticized as being dubious are far more limited than those Aristotle, much less Leibniz and the Absolute Idealists, thought one could reasonably make.

[11] ⌜$A$ is a contingent entity⌝ means the same as ⌜there is an $x$ such that $x$ is identical with $a$ and it is not necessary that there be a $y$ such that $y$ is identical with $x$⌝.

belonging to one category could not have been in any other category or thus failed to possess those characteristics peculiar to their own category. Really interesting essentialistic claims, it could be said, would have to tell us of important essential differences between things of the same general ontological category (e.g., between nightingales and men) or even between things of the same specific kind (between one man and another, for example). Aristotle may have attempted to put forward really interesting essentialistic claims (e.g., that men are essentially men and rational animals), but we have not accepted any such claims, and so have not yet shown the philosophical interest or importance of Essentialism.

At least some of these points are well taken. Perhaps it *is* of no great interest *per se* that I am essentially a being or self or that any given table is essentially a physical body. But that does not mean that Essentialism is philosophically uninteresting or useless. Indeed, Essentialism may have an importance for philosophy that neither defenders nor critics of Essentialism have previously suspected. For it may be that, for one or another general or categorial concept $c$, it is necessarily the case that all and only entities falling under $c$ have a certain, perhaps complex property $e$ essential to them (but not necessary that all and only entities falling under $c$ have $e$ *simpliciter*). In that case we can, perhaps, define the concept $c$, define what it is to fall under $c$, in terms of the concept of being an entity that has $e$ essentially (but cannot define $c$ in terms of the concept of being an entity that has $e$ *simpliciter*). Essentialism *may* not provide essential truths about entities that are interesting in themselves, just because there *may* be no interesting essential truths that distinguish things in the same ontological class or category— assuming, for the moment, that there is some legitimate notion of an ontological class or category. But that very fact indicates a place where Essentialism may well have a major philosophical role to play: in defining various basic general so-called categorial concepts. And it is to this use chiefly that I shall be putting the notion of essence in this book.

# 2. Changes, Processes and Events

## I

The notions of essence and accident (or the *de re* modal notions in terms of which they can be defined) have no place in most definitions of the sort that philosophers have previously attempted or used as examples. Consider, for instance, the putatively innocuous definition of 'brother' as 'male sibling'. It would be a mistake to try to bring the notion of essence into such a definition and define 'brother' as 'male sibling essentially'. For I am a brother, but not essentially a male sibling (or a brother), so that there are cases where the *definiendum* applies, but the *definiens* does not. Indeed, all brothers are only accidentally male siblings (brothers), since any given animal that is a brother (even an identical twin, I think) is (logically) capable of having existed without ever having any siblings. On the other hand, to define 'brother' as 'male sibling accidentally' would be to make an unnecessary and senseless addition to the typical philosophical definition of 'brother'.

Consider, however, the notion of alteration. Of necessity, a thing $x$ alters (or changes, in at least one sense of 'change') if and only if (the way that) $x$ (is) at one time is (to some degree) unlike (the way that) $x$ (is) at another time.[1] It is easy to define

[1] For a similar definition, see T. Penelhum, 'Hume on Personal Identity', *Phil. Review* 64, 1955, p. 580. Incidentally, it is possible to drop phrases like 'the way that . . . is' in stating the conditions of alteration. We can simply talk of a thing $x$ at one time being unlike $x$ at another time. It seems perfectly in order to say, for example, that the Acropolis during the rule of the Turks was almost exactly like (or quite different from) the Acropolis today.

what it is for a thing *to alter* (or *change*) on the above basis; but it is also possible, given the above, to define what it is to be *an alteration* (or *a change*) in (what) something (is like) by use of modal notions *de re*, i.e., by essence and accident. For consider any alteration $y$ that ever occurs in (what) some entity $x$ (is like). $Y$ will essentially exist only if something alters during the history of the universe.[2] It will not be possible for $y$ to exist in a universe where nothing ever alters; or to exist as something other than an alteration; $y$ will be essentially an alteration. If, for example, $y$ is the particular alteration of colour that occurs in a given leaf one autumn, it is impossible that $y$ should have existed even though nothing ever altered or that $y$ should not have been an alteration. Of necessity, then, all alterations are essentially such as to exist only if something (tenselessly) alters. If we also *temporarily* assume that of necessity entities other than alterations at most accidentally exist in a universe where something at some time alters, then we can say that of necessity the concept of (an) alteration applies to all and only entities that essentially: exist only if at some time something alters. But this means that of necessity all and only alterations (in what something is like) are essentially: existent only if there are an $x$, a $t_1$, and a $t_2$ such that $x$ at $t_1$ is to some degree unlike $x$ at $t_2$.[3] And in that case we can offer the following preliminary definition:

'(is) an alteration' means about the same as '(is) essentially: existent only if there are an $x$, a $t_1$ and a $t_2$ such that $x$ at $t_1$ is to some degree unlike $x$ at $t_2$'.

This is an example of definition by essence and accident, of

[2] This is to be understood as saying: '$y$ will essentially be the following: existent only if something alters' or '$y$ will essentially: exist-only-if-something-alters', but not: '$y$ will be a necessary (essential) existent, only if something alters'.

[3] '$t_1$', etc., are temporal variables introduced for the sake of shortening definitions. Note that our use of 'is' and quantifiers will in general be tenseless.

defining some concept (largely) in terms of some combination of claims about what is essential or what is (at most) accidental to entities falling under that concept. Such definition does not recommend itself with regard to the concept of a brother, for one thing because there seems to be nothing that is of necessity essential to all and only brothers. Nor does it seem possible to *avoid* definition by essence and accident with respect to notions like that of (an) alteration. To leave out the 'essentially' in our above definition, for example, would clearly be to invalidate that definition, since everything in the universe (including abstract entities, if there are any) exists only if something alters, given our understanding of 'only if' as having the force of a material conditional. And there is certainly something wrong with any definition that commits us to saying that anything existing in a (possible) world where anything alters is an alteration. Thus because it is clearly not necessary that all and only alterations have the non-modal property of existing only if something alters, definition by essence and accident seems advisable and perhaps unavoidable for the notion of an alteration.[4] And similarly for other, related notions that we shall be discussing here.

We have defined what it is to be an alteration (or change) in what *something or other* is like. Using similar ideas, we can also define what ⌜$b$ is an alteration in (what) $a$ (is like)⌝ means, where $a$ and $b$ are any singular referring expressions. Of necessity, for all $x$, all and only alterations in what $x$ is like are essentially: existent only if $x$ alters, i.e., only if for some $t_1$ and $t_2$, $x$ at $t_1$ is unlike $x$ at $t_2$. So we can temporarily say that:

⌜$b$ is an alteration in (what) $a$ (is like)⌝ means approximately

---

[4] In our definition here we have taken advantage of the fact that all alterations are essentially alterations. But as we shall see below (p. 25f.), some concepts definable by essence and accident can apply accidentally to entities falling under them. That is because definitions by essence and accident need not use only modal predicates and because some (initially quantified) modal predicates can apply accidentally to entities.

the same as ⌜there is an $x$ identical with $a$ such that $b$ essentially: exists only if there are a $t_1$ and a $t_2$ such that $x$ at $t_1$ is unlike $x$ at $t_2$⌝.

This definition and the definition of what it is to be an alteration in general (in what something is like) will both have to be modified below, in the light of certain facts we shall be discussing hereafter. But this much, I think, can be claimed for the two definitions: they contain the kernel of the truth and later qualifications will only be qualifications, not major changes, in what we have said here. (And the same goes for various of the other definitions to be offered in this chapter.)

Now there are many kinds of things that can occur or take place in the universe. Alterations are one sort of thing that can occur. But philosophers have long thought that other kinds of occurrences were possible, indeed actual. For example, the coming into being of one or another entity is something that frequently occurs in the universe; so too the going out of existence (passing away) of various entities. We can use the notion of essence to define the notions of a coming into being and of a going out of existence. For something $x$ to come into being, it has to be the case that at one time $x$ does not exist and at a later time $x$ does. Perhaps, then, we can (for the moment) say that:

'(is) a coming into being' means approximately the same as '(is) essentially: existent only if there are a $t_1$, a $t_2$, and an $x$ such that $t_1$ is before $t_2$ and $x$ exists at $t_2$ and not at $t_1$'.

The notion of a going out of existence or passing away can be defined in parallel fashion.

We should mention, finally, movements and motions. (I shall not here distinguish between these notions.) Of necessity, all motions essentially: exist only if something moves, or (what comes to the same thing) essentially: exist only if two entities are nearer to (or further from) each other at one time than they are at another time. For consider any motion or movement that ever occurs or is occurring; how could *it* have existed if nothing had ever been nearer to (or further from) something else at one time than it was at some other? A given thing that moves may be capable of existing even if nothing ever moves, but the movements it makes are not the sorts of things that (logically or metaphysically) could exist if nothing ever moved. Nor does it make much sense to say that a given movement *m* could in other circumstances have existed as a non-movement. Movements are all essentially movements, and from this it follows that movements all essentially: exist only if something moves. If we temporarily assume, moreover, that of necessity entities other than motions or movements at most only accidentally exist in a universe where there are movements, where things move, then we can offer the following preliminary definition by essence and accident of the notion of a movement (or motion):

'(is) a movement (or motion)' means approximately the same as '(is) essentially: existent only if for some $x$, $y$, $t_1$, and $t_2$, $x$ is nearer to (or further from) $y$ at $t_1$ than at $t_2$'.

It should be clear that this definition works, if at all, only because it uses the notion of essence within it. So we have yet another example of the importance of Essentialism and of the (potential) usefulness of definition by essence and accident.

Our definition of what it is to be a movement or motion is neutral as between the Absolute and Relative Metaphysical Theories of Motion. If the Absolute Theory is true, there are fixed points in space and movement involves something getting nearer to or further from such points; if the Relative Theory is true, then there are no such points, but motion still involves something getting nearer to or further from something else. Thus there is nothing in either theory that goes against our definition of movement or motion.[5]

[5] Definitions of ⌜*a* moves⌝ or of ⌜is a motion of *a*⌝ cannot so easily be framed in a neutral way, For *a*'s referent need not move, even if it gets to

In his *Commonplace Book*,[6] G. E. Moore has claimed that there are only three basic kinds of changes that can occur in the universe: motions, alterations, and comings into being. If Moore is correct—aside from his strange omission of goings out of existence—then we have in effect defined each of the major kinds of changes that can occur in the universe. But Moore's claim also suggests that there is a broader class of things, the class of changes, to which alterations, motions, etc., all of necessity belong, and perhaps we can define the notion of a change by essence and accident if we properly combine our previous definitions of the major kinds of changes there can be. Clearly, Moore treats the notion of (a) change as broader than that of (an) alteration. And it is by no means an uncommon view among philosophers that there is at least one sense of 'change' that includes more than alterations (in what things are like).[7] I am inclined to agree with these philosophers, and believe that we can at least preliminarily define this broad sense of 'change' as follows:

> '(is) a change' means approximately the same as '(is) essentially: existent only if something moves or alters or comes into being or goes out of existence'.

The notion of (a) change can thus be given at least a preliminary

be nearer to another thing; it may just be that the other thing is moving nearer to *a*'s referent, unless some strong version of the Relativistic Theory of Motion is true. Talk of movement in general does not have the problem of committing itself as to which of two entities that are getting nearer to or further from each other is moving.

Our definition of the idea of a movement does not take into account certain possible complications due to Relativity *Physics*. I shall not go into such complications here, but I think they probably could be dealt with within definitions by essence and accident.

[6] *The Commonplace Book of G. E. Moore*, London: Allen and Unwin, 1962, p. 39.

[7] Cf. C. D. Broad in 'Time and Change', *Proc. Arist. Soc. Suppl. Vol.* 8, 1928, p. 180; and J. L. Austin, 'The Meaning of a Word' in *Philosophical Papers*, Oxford: 1961, p. 40.

definition by essence and accident, using only notions that we have already defined or made use of in our previous definitions. (For brevity, we shall use terms previously defined in framing new definitions.)

Someone might at this point object that change is a unitary notion, with something 'common' to all its possible instances, and so cannot properly be defined in a 'disjunctive' manner, as we attempted to do above. But is there really something common to all possible alterations, motions, etc.? I think that those who believe there is would or should want to say that this common element is simply: alteration in what something is like. For it could be held that of necessity whenever something moves, comes into being or ceases to be, this constitutes an alteration at least in what *the universe* is like. If so, then we should not define the notion of a change disjunctively, and, indeed, there is no notion of a change broader than the notion of an alteration (in what something is like). But I am inclined to think there are some possible changes, e.g., movements, that can occur without anything, including the universe, altering. Consider, for example, the instantaneous exchange of place of two exactly similar objects; surely such a change or movement, if possible at all, could occur without there being any alteration in what the universe, or anything else, is like.

It might be objected, however, that such a change or movement is logically impossible, because no one, under any conceivable circumstances, could have any reason to think such a thing had actually occurred. But I wonder whether this kind of Verificationism can be effectively used nowadays in the service of a claim of logical impossibility, considering the faults or counterexamples that have been found with respect to practically every verificationistic Principle of Verifiability. Consider, for example, such claims as 'no (animate) being or self ever exists' or 'there are never any beings capable of having any reasons to believe anything'. It is hard to imagine how such claims could ever be supported by reasons or reasonably believed, yet they seem clearly meaningful and only contingently false. Moreover, there are logically possible circumstances of various 'strange' kinds in which, I think, there would be evidence for and reason to believe the claim that instantaneous change of place had taken place between two exactly similar objects. The evidence would be indirect and of a sort not obtainable, perhaps, in the actual world, but it would be valid nonetheless. In particular, it would, I think, be possible to use a reliable soothsayer, magic wand, or confirmation machine to obtain such evidence of instant exchange of place, but I shall not go into the details of such cases here, for reasons of space and because such cases have been described at length elsewhere.[8] In any event, Verificationism does not seem to provide much of an argument against the possibility of instantaneous change of place on the part of exactly similar objects.

However, it might be held that even if two objects could instantaneously exchange their locations, such an exchange would involve or be an alteration in what the universe was like, since the universe would come to possess a property it had previously lacked, e.g., the property of having object $a$ at place $p$, or near object $b$. But there is a difference between having different properties at different times and altering. A thing $s$ may be one year old at one time and two years old a year later and thus have, on the philosopher's notion of a property, different properties at different times; but it hardly follows that (the way) $s$ (is) at a year old is to any degree unlike (the way) $s$ (is) at two years old, or thus that $s$ has to any degree altered over the year.[9] (I assume that the notion of alteration marches with that of unlikeness, not with that of mere acquisition of new

[8] See my *Reason and Scepticism*, London: Allen and Unwin, 1970, pp. 25ff., 46; and E. Erwin, 'The Confirmation Machine' in *Boston Studies in the Philosophy of Science* VIII, pp. 306–21.

[9] For discussion of similar points, see *Reason and Scepticism*, Ch. 5, sect. 2, where it is argued that two entities can be exactly alike at a time even though they have different past histories, and so have different properties, and where I defend the legitimacy of the whole notion of exact likeness (exact similarity) against some of its critics.

properties.) We have thus seen no reason to think that instant exchange of place is impossible or that such exchange would have to be accompanied by alteration on the part of the universe or anything else. So I am inclined to think that change is not a unitary notion, with something common to all its possible instances, and to think that that notion can properly be defined disjunctively.

Nonetheless, our definition of what it is to be a change faces a problem arising from the fact that not every coming into being or going out of existence is a clear case of a change even in the broad sense of the term we are attempting to define. For if it is now time *t*, then one might claim that *t* exists now but at no other time. But then it would seem that times both come into and go out of existence. On our definition, any coming into being or going out of existence is a change, but is it reasonable to hold that comings into being or goings out of existence of times constitute real *changes* that *take place* in the universe, real *events*, for instance? (Of course, there may be something wrong with the idea of times' going out of or coming into existence, in which case the present challenge to our definition of change would collapse. I shall not dispute the possibility of times' coming to be or ceasing to be, however, if only because the assumption of such a possibility makes things harder for our definition of change.) It is an old, but not undisputed, view that the mere passage of time does not in and of itself constitute the occurrence of changes or events.[10] But this view is controversial, and there are many philosophers who have held that the (mere) passage of time does logically involve (necessitate) change, in the sense that there could not conceivably be a 'frozen' or static universe in which time passed. For such philosophers, time entails the existence of real goings on or changes in the world. Now if these philosophers are correct, then perhaps the coming into and going out of existence of times should be considered real changes that take place in the universe, since such comings into and goings out of existence would

[10] Cf. S. Shoemaker, 'Time Without Change', *J. Phil.* 66, 1969, p. 364.

presumably essentially: exist only when there were various real changes occurring, and since what thus logically involves change might safely be considered itself to be a change.[11] And in that case, there would be no reason (as yet) to modify our definition of the notion of a change.

However, philosophers who claim that time without (real) change is logically impossible typically back up that claim with some sort of Verificationist argument about the impossibility of ever having reason to think that there (tenselessly) is a passage of time without any real changes occurring. We have already seen the vulnerability of the assumption that some sort of verifiability is required in order for something to be logically possible, so we have no particular reason to think any Verificationist argument will have any force in showing that time without change is impossible. Furthermore, it has been argued by S. Shoemaker that it is in fact *possible* to have inductive reason to believe in the passage of time without there being any events or changes. In 'Time Without Change', Shoemaker describes in detail a logically possible situation where he thinks people would have reasons of scientific simplicity to think that one part of the world 'froze' for a year every three years, another part for a year every four years, the remaining part for a year every five years, and all three parts together for a whole year every sixty years.[12] I shall not go into Shoemaker's actual arguments, but I do believe that those arguments make it clear that time without change is verifiable or confirmable, or at least, make it clear that arguments very similar to Shoemaker's could be used to show this. I think, then, that no one has ever given any good reason to hold that time without change is impossible, and I am, moreover, inclined to think that if time without change is logically possible, then it is

[11] This is especially true in the light of our discussion of the conditions of identity in Chapter 5, below. The notion of logical involvement is equivalent to the notion of logical dependence defined later in this chapter.

[12] *Loc. cit.*

also logically possible for time to pass without there *ever* being any changes.

But if we accept the possibility of time passing without there ever being any changes, then the coming into and going out of existence of times—if, indeed, such a thing is possible—must be held not to involve any ordinary changes occurring in the universe. And since the mere passage of time does not, I think, count as (a) change of any sort in the ordinary broad sense of the word 'change'—a frozen universe, after all, being one of which it is natural to say that nothing happens and no changes take place in it—we must alter our definition of the notion of a change. For on that definition, the mere coming into being or going out of existence of a time counts as a change.

This can most easily be done, perhaps, by saying that:

'(is) a change' means something like '(is) essentially: existent only if something *other than a time* moves or alters or comes into being or goes out of existence'.

This definition will require adjustment later (pp. 33f., 103f.). But it does eliminate the coming into and going out of existence of times as cases of changes,[13] while still including as changes the sorts of things one is inclined to think of as real changes in the broad sense of the term. Thus we have used the concepts 'alters' and 'moves', etc., to define preliminarily the very general notion of a change. We can now use the notion of a change to define two other important notions: that of an event and that of a process.

## II

Intuitively, the notion of an event seems close to that of a change, in the broad sense of 'change' that we have been defining and that has been much used by philosophers. Most of the

[13] Assuming that there are such entities at all; but if there are not, our definition will at worst, I think, be redundant, not incorrect.

changes occurring in the universe that one thinks of are also events. And every genuine event counts as a genuine change as well. But some possible changes are not events, namely, those that have infinite duration. If, for example, there were a rocket ship that had been travelling for an infinite amount of time in the past, its infinitely long trip or motion would not, I think, constitute an event, even if that trip or motion eventually came to an end. On the other hand, I think there is nothing in the notions of a process and of a change to preclude infinitely long processes and changes. For example, it seems to make perfectly good sense to speak of an infinitely long *process* of evolutionary *change*, in a way that it does not sound correct to speak of an infinitely long evolutionary *event*. We might, then, offer the following *final* definition of eventhood (final definitions here will always be signalled by an asterisk):

*'(is) an event' means approximately the same as '(is) a change such that there is a $t_1$ before any $t_2$ when it exists and a $t_3$ after any $t_4$ when it exists'.[14]

Someone might object that our definition allows events of arbitrarily long finite duration. And normally we do not describe million-year what-have-you's as events, and apply 'event' only to events that take a relatively short time. However, from a great enough temporal perspective, even what takes thousands or millions of years can stand out as an event and be considered such. Renan in his *Life of Jesus* (Chapter 1) speaks of the conversion of much of the world to Christianity as a great event of world history; and an evolutionary biologist, whose perspective is that of the whole development of life on Earth, will quite unself-consciously speak of the development of jaws, for example, as an 'event of great evolutionary progress', even though it took millions of years for that development to take

---

[14] I assume that at all times when an event is occurring or occurs, it *exists* or there *is* something identical with it. But it is often *odd* to talk of the *existence* of events.

place.[15] Given these facts about usage of the word 'event', I am inclined to think that events can be arbitrarily (finitely) long. For it seems plausible to hold, with respect to such very general and metaphysically central concepts as that of an event, that it is analytic of such concepts that they apply *simpliciter*, whenever they apply *sub specie aeternitatis*.

So far we have mentioned only the term 'event', not the term 'occurrence'. The latter is ambiguous in a way that the former is not, for in one sense we can speak of there being three occurrences of the word 'anent' on a certain page, and there is no similar usage of the word 'event'. There is a sense in which 'occurrence' just means 'instance' and applies to entities other than events. In another sense of the term, however, 'occurrence' means the same as 'event' and can be defined in the way we defined 'event' just above.

The notion of a process, we have seen, differs from that of an event, inasmuch as there can be processes of infinite duration, but no such events. Also it makes sense to talk of instantaneous events, but not of instantaneous processes. Perhaps we can at least preliminarily define the notion of a process by essence and accident, making use of these facts. We can say that:

'(is) a process' means approximately the same as '(is) a change that is essentially: existent only if (at least) two temporally non-overlapping changes exist'.

This definition does not exclude non-continuous processes, since it seems to make perfectly good sense to speak of temporarily halting or interrupting a process. Nor does the definition exclude the possibility of irregular, disorderly, purposeless, or accidental processes. There may be a narrow sense of the term in which processes have to be orderly or purposeful, but surely there is also in English a broad sense of the term in which, for example, we can naturally speak of disorderly,

[15] See N. Holton III, *The Evidence of Evolution*, N.Y.: American Heritage, 1968, p. 75.

inexplicable or random processes. Our definition, furthermore, commits us to calling something a process even if it involves just two temporally separate changes. And this might seem strange. It is clearly wrong to speak of a single instantaneous change or alteration as a process. And it is also true that we less frequently (and even perhaps less willingly) speak of something composed of two successive changes or events as a process than we speak of something composed of five or ten changes or events as a process. But I still think that in the right circumstances educated speakers of English will apply the term 'process' to something occurring in just two stages. Thus H. W. Fowler, in *Modern English Usage*, writes of 'the process of first noticing that *as well as* means nearly the same as *besides,* and then giving it a wrong construction that would be right for *besides*'.[16] In the light of such usage, I think our definition of 'process' is not implausible, or at least, is not clearly inaccurate, as a first approximation.

Our definition of processhood commits us to saying that a series of changes other than alterations qualifies as a process. But there is also the expression 'process of alteration', which applies only to series of alterations. We can say that:

'(is) a process of alteration in what something is like' means approximately the same as '(is) essentially: existent only if there are an *x*, a $t_1$, a $t_2$, and a $t_3$ such that *x* at $t_1$ is unlike *x* at $t_2$ and *x* at $t_2$ is unlike *x* at $t_3$ and $t_2$ is between $t_1$ and $t_3$, i.e., essentially: existent only if there are two temporally non-overlapping alterations in (what) something *x* (is like).[17]

We can in similar fashion define ⌜*a* is a process of alteration in *b*⌝.

Our definition also commits us to holding that processes are essentially processes. And there are problems with such a view.

[16] Oxford: Clarendon, 1930, article on 'well', p. 703.

[17] Our definition does not require *x* at $t_1$ to be unlike *x* at $t_3$, so as not to exclude cyclical processes of alteration.

Consider, to begin with, leaf $a$'s gradually turning brown. If there is such an entity as leaf $a$'s gradually turning brown (and we shall discuss what such entities are like, if they exist, in Chapter 5), it is not identical with the gradual change of colour (to brown) that occurs in $a$ on a given occasion, if we think of the former as something that (logically) can occur many times, but of the latter as an unrepeatable instance of the former. (Deeper reasons for this denial of identity will emerge in Chapters 4 and 5.) But whatever $a$'s gradually turning brown is, it is clearly a process, something incapable of existing unless two temporally non-overlapping changes occur. And, further, it essentially meets these conditions, is essentially a process. The same, I think, is true of the unrepeatable gradual change in colour that occurs in $a$ during some stretch of time. However, consider: $a$'s changing from green to brown. One could hold that such a change would be a process, if $a$ gradually changed from green to brown, but that it would not be a process if $a$ were on only a single occasion to change instantaneously from green to brown. One might, in other words, hold that $a$'s changing from green to brown could take time and thus be a process, or else occur instantaneously and in that case not count as a process. But then there would be processes that were only accidentally processes, and our previous definition would be mistaken. But is this a correct way to understand $a$'s changing from green to brown? Could one not argue that when $a$ changes gradually from green to brown, $a$'s changing from green to brown is a change that occurs by means of certain processes (e.g., $a$'s unrepeatable gradual change from green to red), but is not itself a process, since it could have existed (taken place) even if there had been no such processes, and so does not logically involve there being such processes? On such a view, $a$'s changing from green to brown could never be a process, because it could never be more than causally dependent on processes,[18] and nothing

[18] Subject to certain qualifications to be introduced in the next section of this chapter.

could be accidentally a process.[19] I cannot see my way clear to deciding between these two ways of looking at $a$'s changing from green to brown. If the latter way is correct, then our definition of processhood need not be modified, at least for the moment. If the former way is correct, modification of the definition is clearly necessary. And perhaps the required modification can be effected by adding to our earlier definition of processhood in such a way that it reads:

'(is) a process' means something like '(is) a change that is essentially: existent only if (at least) two temporally non-overlapping changes exist, or (is) a change such that there are (at least) two temporally non-overlapping changes $x$ and $y$ such that it essentially exists only if $x$ and $y$ (tenselessly) exist'.

(A process will not depend on the two non-overlapping changes, however, since on my usage some $u$ logically depends on some $v$ just if $u$ essentially exists *only when* $v$ does.) Given this addition, $a$'s changing from green to brown counts as a process if it takes time. For in such a case the following two changes will exist: $a$'s losing its greenness and $a$'s attaining brownness. $A$'s changing from green to brown essentially exists only if each of these exists; and in a situation where $a$ gradually or non-instantaneously changes from green to brown, these two changes will exist but not overlap each other temporally. E.g., if $a$ changes from green to red to brown, $a$'s losing its greenness will occur and be over before $a$ attains brownness, and so before $a$'s attaining brownness. Thus it is possible to alter our definition of processhood so as to allow for accidental processes, if it is necessary or advisable to do so. But at present the issue whether the original or modified definition of processhood is preferable is, it seems to me, very much up in the air.

[19] In any case, events are not always essentially events. A given masked ball that ends at midnight only accidentally does not go on forever. Certain instantaneous events, on the other hand, may be essentially instantaneous, and essentially events.

Furthermore, this uncertainty makes it also unclear whether processes and events exhaust the realm of changes that could occur in the universe. For consider the motion (moving) of matter in the void. If there is such an entity, it is a change by our definition; but if it goes on for an infinite amount of time, it is not an event. However, this change, the moving of matter in the void, only accidentally does not take place all at once, and so is not a process according to our original definition of processhood, even when it goes on for an infinite amount of time. So if that original definition is correct in ruling out accidental processes, some possible changes are neither processes nor events.

There is also some problem as to whether all events and processes really should count as changes, as our definitions imply. We can speak of a given masked ball that occurs on a given night as an event, e.g., as the social event of the year. But on our definitions, every event is a change (in the broad sense of the term), and it seems odd to call a masked ball a change. Of course, one might claim that this oddness results from and is a sign of the breaking of a linguistic rule, but one might also want to say, instead, that the oddness is merely due to the fact that we rarely (need to) call masked balls changes, since we have the more specific word 'event' to apply to them, and that in fact masked balls *are* changes.[20]

This latter tack derives sustenance from the fact that when a masked ball occurs, genuine changes do take place in the universe (and on the earth). Hands get dirty, people get nearer to or further from each other, dresses tear, etc., and surely each of these occurrences constitutes a genuine change in the way things are that occurs in our part of the universe. Indeed, there could not have been a masked ball, and any given masked ball could not have existed, unless it had been made up of such changes, unless such changes had occurred as part of it.

---

[20] Cf. J. Fodor, *Psychological Explanation*, N.Y.: Random House, 1968, pp. 100ff.

Actually, we might well consider a masked ball to *be* some sort of complex of genuine changes, and if we consider a complex *of* events (like a masked ball) to be a (complex) event itself, why not consider a complex of changes to be itself a complex (or complicated or compound) change? Think, for example, of other, perhaps simpler, complexes of changes (or events) that occur in the universe. If one part of an object $x$ changes from green to red, while another part changes from brown to blue, and if thereafter both parts change to purple and then to orange, a complex series of events or changes has taken place in the universe, and in $x$ in particular. And it seems natural to say that the change of one part of $x$ from green to red is part of a larger, more complex change (or process of change) that occurs in $x$, and in the universe, because it is natural to think of a series or complex of changes as itself a change of a complex or complicated sort. But if so, why not consider the complex of changes (or events) that makes up a masked ball to constitute a very complex sort of change in some broad ordinary sense of the word, just as in fact we do consider it to constitute a complex sort of event?[21]

[21] According to G. E. Moore (*Commonplace Book*, p. 85), two disparate events, processes, etc., in different parts of the universe need not themselves be part of some single event, process, or change. From a large enough perspective, however, I am inclined to think that even two distant and causally unrelated events can be thought of as constituting a single complex event, or process, or change, and so perhaps *do* constitute a single complex event, or process, or change. After all, many philosophers have thought that any two distant and causally unrelated objects $x$ and $y$ together constitute a single scattered entity $z$. But then if $x$ changes colour while $y$ shrinks, can we not speak of a (scattered) change taking place in $z$? If two disparate distant events, etc., *cannot* correctly be thought of as together constituting a single entity (possibly involving change in some scattered object), then they will not consitute a single event, etc., or a single entity with such and such an essence, and neither the *definiens* nor the *definiendum* of any of our definitions will apply. And if two disparate distant events, etc., *do* constitute a single entity, then that entity will presumably be an event, etc. (happening, perhaps, to some scattered object), and will meet our definitions of 'event', etc. So there seems to be

On the other hand, these considerations may just be misguided in some way I cannot see. It may just be that not every event is a change in any *ordinary* broad sense of the term. If so, there may not be any *single* ordinary word that applies to everything that can occur or be occurring and that can be defined as we have defined the putative broad sense of 'change' above. But even so, there will still be the expression 'change or complex of changes', and this complex expression in its ordinary sense will apply to anything that takes place or is taking place at any time in the universe, and can, I think, be defined as we have defined 'change' in its putative broad sense. Furthermore, even if there is no such broad sense of 'change' in ordinary English, philosophers (e.g., Shoemaker, *op. cit.*) have often used the word 'change' in that broad sort of way (but in such a way as to exclude mere changes of time, for example, as genuine changes). And I think we have above at least defined a common broad philosophical notion of change. In addition, such a sense of 'change' has at least in the past had some currency in ordinary usage. *The Book of Common Prayer*, for example, speaks of 'the sundry and manifold changes of the world', thereby indicating a notion of change that would seem to apply to anything that ever occurs or is occurring. But even if such a usage of the term 'change' is no longer extant in common parlance, there is such a usage among philosophers, and it is important from a metaphysical standpoint to understand and, if possible, to define that usage of 'change'. This we have attempted to do here.

## III

I would like now to consider whether and why physical objects or bodies like tables, flowers, lakes, and human bodies are *not* processes, events, etc. Many philosophers have either been convinced that physical objects or bodies like tables were

no need, at the moment, to change our current definitions of 'process', 'event', etc.

really events, or processes, etc.—and perhaps not 'objects' or 'bodies' at all—or have thought there was no significant difference between physical bodies and processes, events, etc. In *Scientific Thought*,[22] for example, C. D. Broad maintains that the white cliffs of Dover are just a very boring kind of event. Russell in *Philosophy*[23] holds that anything of short duration is an event. In *Experience and Nature*,[24] John Dewey says that every existence (existing thing) is an event. In *The Structure of Appearance*,[25] Nelson Goodman has claimed that things are just monotonous events. And, finally, the view that all things are *processes* is sometimes attributed to Heraclitus[26] and Engels.[27]

The major impetus to such thinking seems to be the belief that all bodies are constantly in flux, subject to innumerable internal and external changes, and thus so involved with changes, processes, and events that at least in a world like ours there is no difference between processes, etc., and entities like tables, lakes, etc. But despite the large number of philosophers who have held that so-called physical bodies are processes or events, there have been other philosophers who have disagreed with this sort of view. In his *Commonplace Book*,[28] for example, G. E. Moore says that it is a mistake to call such things as an arm or a desk occurrences or events. And Margaret Macdonald defends the view that such things as tables are not processes against Engel's claims to the contrary.[29] It is not hard to see why some philosophers have been bothered by the claim that ordinary objects like tables are really not 'objects' at all, but

[22] N.Y.: Harcourt, Brace, and World, 1923, p. 393.

[23] N.Y.: Norton, 1927, pp. 276ff.

[24] N.Y.: Norton, 1929, pp. 70f.

[25] Cambridge: Harvard, 1951, first edition, p. 357.

[26] E.g., by K. Popper in *Conjectures and Refutations*, N.Y.: Basic Books, 1962, pp. 136–65.

[27] E.g., by Margaret Macdonald in 'Things and Processes' in M. Macdonald, ed., *Philosophy and Analysis*, N.Y.: Basic Books 1954

[28] p. 85.

[29] *Op. cit., passim.*

processes or events. Such claims go against the ordinary man's application of 'process', 'event', 'change', etc. And it sounds odd to the native ear to hear a table called a process or an event. Such oddness gives us some reason at least to suspect the view that tables, etc., are processes or events, and we will have still more reason to doubt or deny that view if we can frame otherwise plausible definitions of 'process', 'event', etc., from which the falsity of that view can easily be seen to follow (given certain fairly obvious background assumptions). Unfortunately, we have not yet produced such definitions. For on our definitions as they stand many tables, lakes, flowers, etc., would count as processes, or events, etc. Let us see why this is so.

I mentioned earlier my acceptance of the view that the particular entities out of which something $x$ emerges have something important to do with which particular thing $x$ is. This is, in fact, an aspect of a more general fact about the individuation of entities, the fact, namely, that which particular entity something is is intimately connected with how that thing was brought about or caused to exist. And just as it would seem that I could not have originated in totally different matter, it does not seem possible that I should have existed without in any way having been caused to come into existence. If a being in some other galaxy had come from a sperm and egg exactly like but not materially identical with those I in fact came from and had grown up to be exactly similar in character and physical nature to me, as I in fact am today, that being would not have been me, the Slote my friends refer to, even if nothing like me as I in fact am and have been had existed on Earth. Similarly, if the sperm and egg I came from had never come together and if a being exactly like me as I was when I first existed (or like me today) had suddenly sprung into existence, complete with all its matter, by total causal accident, that being would not have been *me*. In such a situation there is nothing to make the being that springs into existence count as me, rather than simply as just like me. And for much the same reason, finally, if the sperm and egg from which I came had never come together (or even existed), and if instead there had always existed a being like me as I now am, a being with hazel eyes, short fingers, etc., who had been 'frozen' or static from all eternity with just those features, that being would not have been me. Because of the role one's origins play in one's individuation, I am essentially: an entity that is caused to come into existence, and so essentially: do not exist from all eternity, am not infinite in the past.

In that case, I and most other things meet our earlier definitions of 'change', 'process', and 'event'. For if I essentially do not exist from all eternity, then I essentially exist only if at some time something alters or moves or ceases to be, etc.[30] But this does not show that I and other things are really processes, etc. Our previous definitions may be in error, and the fact that it is odd to speak of tables, people, etc., as processes gives us some reason to think that this is so. If, furthermore, we can add to our earlier definitions so as to rule out tables, etc., as processes, changes, etc., that will show that there really is a difference between what we normally consider to be processes, etc., and what we normally consider not to be processes, etc. And that will give us strong reason to think that tables, etc., are not processes, etc., and to believe in the accuracy of our amended definitions of processhood, etc.

We have argued that I, who am finite in the past, am essentially so. But if there were any beings who had existed from all eternity, they would for similar reasons presumably be essentially infinite in the past, essentially existent from all eternity, if existent at all. Presumably a being essentially infinite in the past and a being essentially finite in the past could at a given time exactly resemble one another, despite their dissimilar pasts. And in particular there could have been a being very

[30] It might be thought that I could have avoided the problem of ruling out tables, etc., as changes, etc., if I had defined 'alteration' as 'something that essentially: exists only if something alters at some time *when it exists*' and had done similar things with my definitions of motion, etc. As far as I can tell, however, such a technique of defining these concepts gets into other, serious difficulties that there is no space to mention here.

similar to me as I in fact was when I first existed that existed in causal isolation 'frozen' from all eternity *up until* the first moment of my existence.[31] Such a being might then have started changing in exactly the way I began to change when I first existed, so that at every moment of my existence it was exactly like me. But, of course, if there had been such a being in a frozen or static state from all eternity, that being (logically or metaphysically) could have continued to exist without ever leaving that state. And if so, then that being presumably could have existed without anything ever altering, moving, etc. For if the being really had existed in causal isolation from all eternity, and had only started to interact with things at the moment when I came into existence, then surely the existence of that being would have to be logically independent of changes occurring in other parts of the universe, so that that being would not be essentially: existent only if something (other than a time) moves, alters, etc., at some time or other. In the light of the above, then, we can perhaps modify our definition of 'motion' and say that:

'(is) a motion' means approximately the same as '(is) an entity $x$ such that $x$ essentially exists only if something moves and such that it is not possible that for all $t$ and $t'$ when $x$ exists, there is something $y$ not identical with $x$ that is exactly like $x$ between and/or at $t$ and $t'$ and that is not essentially existent only if something moves'.[32]

This definition eliminates me, my body, tables, and lakes as motions (or movements), since even if I am essentially existent only if some things move in causing me to exist, it is possible

[31] In 'Time and Change', p. 176, Broad also accepts the possibility of frozen or static existence.

[32] The definition is so phrased as to exclude not only temporally finite non-motions like us, but also non-motions with infinite past existence. For simplicity, I have stated the definition without spelling out the meaning of 'something moves' the way I did previously.

that there be, between (or at) any $t$ and $t'$ when I exist, something exactly like me between (or at) $t$ and $t'$ that existed from all eternity and could have existed even if nothing ever moved. But it is impossible for any motion not to meet the amended definition, because for any possible motion $m$, it is necessary that if $m$ is exactly resembled by something between (or at) any $t$ and $t'$ when $m$ exists, one of the entities thus resembling $m$ will be a movement that we can no more conceive to exist in a world without movement, than we can conceive $m$ existing in such a world.

Our definitions of 'alteration' and 'change' must be modified in similar fashion. For example, we should now say that:

'(is) an alteration' has approximately the same meaning as '(is) an entity $x$ such that $x$ essentially exists only if something alters and such that it is not possible that for all $t$ and $t'$ when $x$ exists, there exists something $y$ not identical with $x$ that is exactly like $x$ between and/or at $t$ and $t'$ and that is not essentially existent only if something alters'.

We can keep our definitions of the terms 'event' and 'occurrence' as they now stand—though of course they will have different force from previously. The definition of 'process', however, will have to be altered, for much the same reason that our definitions of 'motion', etc., had to be changed. This is easily done, and I shall not go into the details here. (However, because comings into being, or goings out of existence, of times, if they occur, may well be genuine comings into being, or goings out of existence, it would at this point probably be difficult, if not impossible, to offer plausible revised definitions of '(is) a coming into being', or '(is) a going out of existence'. Fortunately, this need not, I think, interfere with the completion of our other definitions by essence and accident.)

Our present definitions, let us hope, accord with ordinary beliefs about what entities count as processes or events at the same time that they allow us to see what distinguishes tables and other bodies from the sorts of things we ordinarily think of as processes or events. Thus assuming the accuracy of the definitions enables us plausibly to *explain why* the things we normally do not call processes, etc., are *not* processes, etc. And all this stands in favour of the accuracy of our definitions and against the common philosophical thesis that tables, lakes, etc., are in fact events, processes, changes, etc.[33]

Actually, it does not analytically follow from our definitions that tables, etc., are not processes, etc. It is rather just that if our definitions are correct, and if certain common assumptions about tables are true, then tables are not processes, etc. One such assumption, I think, is that the tables that actually exist in the world are (logically) capable of being entirely static, or at least are (logically) capable of being exactly resembled by possible static or frozen entities. We are inclined to make such an assumption, if at all, because we think that however much the submicroscopic particles of matter that make up a table are in motion and changing, those particles can clearly and distinctly be imagined to be frozen in place and changeless, with the table they constitute continuing to exist in a frozen or static form. If such a thing is possible, then I think tables do not meet our definitions of 'process', 'event', etc., and do not count as processes, events, etc.[34] But if such a thing is impossible—

---

[33] Our definitions do not preclude the possibility of borderline cases of processes, etc., however. It may be not only uncertain but also indeterminate whether, e.g., lightning flashes are or have to be *flashings* or *swarmings* (of electrons) that could not (be resembled by things that could) exist in the absence of all change. I assume there can be borderline cases of modal concepts. Consider the fact that if a given shade of colour is a borderline case of redness, it will presumably also be a borderline case with respect to the property of *possibly* being a shade of red and the property of *essentially* being a shade of red.

[34] Consider, however, the following argument to show that tables, etc., are events and processes on our present definitions: (a) tables are essentially composed of atoms, and (b) it is necessary that *atoms* move in certain specified lawful ways. So tables cannot be (resembled by possible) static things and are events and processes. But if atoms are particles, and particles are entities that can cease to move, then given (b), atoms are not

say, because tables and even 'particles' are all ultimately 'composed' of events and processes—then tables, people, lakes and the like may all turn out to be events and processes.

Our original definitions of 'change', etc., ran into difficulty because various people and tables are essentially not infinite in the past. Indeed, it follows from what we have been saying that any being or table, etc., that either had a causal origin or simply sprang into existence would be essentially non-infinite in the past. And, by a similar token, any entity that existed from all eternity would be essentially an entity with infinite past existence. These facts can now be of *help* to us in defining (away) two other metaphysically important notions: the notions of the future and of the past.

I am a conscious being who in fact has existed only finitely in the (temporal direction of the) past. And I am essentially so. But now consider the future. I shall in fact die and cease to exist (I assume), and so, barring miracles of science, will every other being that ever exists. But it is not essential to me that I should thus perish; I am logically capable of existing forever; and this is true of all creatures that ever exist. We are all at most accidentally finite in the (temporal direction of the) future. Of course, even if there are no beings that will never cease to exist, there might have been. But even such beings would not have been essentially such as to exist forever in the future. Of necessity, any conscious being that exists infinitely into the future only accidentally does so.[35] And all the above holds as

essentially atoms. And in that case (a) seems to be false too; tables will at most only be essentially composed of *particles*. The more reason there is to believe (b), the more implausible (a) becomes; and so the argument being considered does not go through. Incidentally, there are arguments similar to the one just considered that attempt to show the impossibility of an object's changing, say, from silver to wood and that can be criticized along the lines we have just indicated.

[35] I am not unhappy to be thus committed to the impossibility of a necessarily existent God. It is hard to understand how a platonic universal or number could cease to be, but with beings I think it is always *imaginable* that they should perish, however great and wonderful they may be. If God

much for physical bodies as it does for conscious beings, and for the same reasons.

If all this is so, then the past histories of physical bodies and (animate) beings or selves stand under much more stringent logical requirements than the future histories of such entities.[36] And the above-cited facts about the way beings and bodies are essentially different with respect to future and past are, I would like to claim, definitive of the difference between future and past as temporal directions (from the present or from any other given time). That is, I think we can provide a contextual definition of 'the past' and 'the future' by means of concepts that we have already used, and the notions of physical body and of self or being (which we shall be defining later on), plus the concept of existing nearer or further in a temporal direction.

*⌜$a$ is the temporal direction of the past⌝ means approximately the same as ⌜there is an $x$ identical with $a$ such that $x$ is a temporal direction and such that of necessity any being or physical body $y$ is such that if there is a $t_1$ further in $x$ than any $t_2$ when $y$ exists, then $y$ is essentially such that there exists a $t_1$ further in $x$ than any $t_2$ when $y$ exists; and if there is no $t_1$ further in $x$ than any $t_2$ when $y$ exists, then $y$ is essentially such that there is no $t_1$ further in $x$ than any $t_2$ when $y$ exists⌝.

I think we conceive the future to be opposed or contrary to the past, not just the negation of the past. So we should not just define the notion of the future by putting in a negation sign before the words 'of necessity' in the above definition of the (temporal direction of the) past. I think we can best capture

is supposed to be a logically imperishable *being*, one has, I think, combined incompatible qualities. For insight as to why theologians tried to combine such incompatible qualities in a single entity, see Sartre, *Being and Nothingness*, N.Y.: Phil. Library, 1956, pp. 565ff.

[36] But not the past histories of substances like gold or kinds like the kind gold ring. These entities, if they exist, are accidentally finite (or infinite) in the past because not individuated by their origins. The reasons for this will become clearer in Ch. 5.

the opposedness of the future to the past in our definition of the future by saying:

*⌜$a$ is the temporal direction of the future⌝ means approximately the same as ⌜there is an $x$ identical with $a$ such that $x$ is a temporal direction and such that of necessity any being or physical body $y$ is such that if there is a $t_1$ further in $x$ than any $t_2$ when $y$ exists, then $y$ is accidentally such that there is a $t_1$ further in $x$ than any $t_2$ when $y$ exists; and if there is no $t_1$ further in $x$ than any $t_2$ when $y$ exists, then $y$ is accidentally such that there is no $t_1$ further in $x$ than any $t_2$ when $y$ exists⌝.

These final definitions allow us to define away the notions of pastness and futureness in terms of notions we have been and shall be defining, plus the additional temporal notion of being nearer or further in a temporal direction. And of course our definitions are definitions by essence and accident. Given the definitions, furthermore, there is a great difference between future and past, and there is real force to the traditional philosophical thesis that the future is the realm of freedom and possibility and the past the realm of constraint and necessity. For it follows from our definitions that bodies and beings or selves are logically free with respect to their existence in the future in a way that they are not free with respect to their existence in the past.

It should be noted, however, that the correctness of our definitions depends on the logical impossibility of certain kinds of time travel into the past (though not necessarily on the impossibility of past causation in general). If certain sorts of Relativistic time travel are possible, then it may well be that $x$ is finite in the past but that it is also possible that $x$ should have been sent back in a time machine in such a way as to exist at all past times. In other words, someone's world line may not in fact bend back on itself just because he never enters a time machine; but that being could have entered a time machine and his world line could have bent back on itself, and he could have been sent back to exist at every previous time (i.e., his world line could turn back on itself towards the past and never end or turn back on itself again).[37] If such time travel is possible and a being can be accidentally finite (or infinite) in the past, our definition of the past will be in error, and we will possess no means to distinguish past from future by essence and accident.

I am not sure that such time travel is impossible, but I think the whole idea of it is very suspicious and hard to make sense of. For one thing, I think that time travel of the sort just described is only possible if it is possible for a self or animate being to be in two places at once; for if one is sent back in a time machine, it will presumably have to be possible for one to be located in a time machine (going towards the past) and outside a time machine (going towards the future) at one and the same time. And I find this idea so hard to understand, that I think there are excellent grounds for doubting the possibility of time travel into the (infinite) past and for thinking that our definitions by essence and accident of the notions of the future and the past may well be correct.

[37] Cf. H. Putnam, 'It Ain't Necessarily So', *J. Phil.* 62, 1959, for a description of this kind of time travel.

# 3. Conscious Beings

## I

In Chapter 2, I offered definitions of concepts like process, event, change, motion, alteration, coming into being, going out of existence, future, and past. These concepts (except for the last two) are the same as or very close to those that Aristotle sought to explicate and/or define in the *Physics*. But our attempts at definition were crucially different from Aristotle's. For although Aristotle makes use of the notions of essence and accident in the *Physics*, he does not use those notions as the basis for his definitions or explanations of motion, change, and the like. But this difference is extremely important. For I think such notions as change, motion, and the like only *can* be accurately defined via definition by essence and accident;[1] thus I look upon the previous chapter as an attempt to fulfil or carry further the enterprise begun by Aristotle in the *Physics*: firstly, because I attempted in Chapter 2 to analyse notions like those Aristotle attempted to analyse in the *Physics* and, secondly, because in doing so I made use of the basically Aristotelian notions of essence (necessity *de re*) and accident (possibility *de re*) in a way that Aristotle himself, it seems, never thought to use them.

The definitions of last chapter were based on only four primitive (i.e., undefined) notions or clusters of notions. First, they in-

---

[1] Aristotle's own definitions in *Physics* III, chs. 1 and 2, strike one as circular in a blatant way; an alteration, for example, is supposed to be the fulfillment of a potential for altering. Also, what about uncaused alterations?

volved the strictly logical concepts of quantification theory (with identity): existential quantification, negation, conjunction, etc., and, of course, identity. Second, various spatio-temporal notions like Time, times, Space, points in space, before, after, nearer, further, at (a time), at (a place), etc. In the third place, our definitions used the notion of exact likeness (or, what I take to be the same things: exact resemblance and exact similarity). And fourth and finally, the definitions that we offered crucially involved the notions of essence and accident (necessity *de re* and possibility *de re*).

Definition by essence and accident has been useful in defining what it is to be a change, in defining various subcategories of changes, and in explaining the difference between changes and non-changes. But definition by essence and accident can be put to use in a totally different area where definitions are sought; it can be used to define what it is to be an (animate) being (as we shall attempt to do in the present chapter), and also to define the notion of a physical entity (in Chapters 4 and 5) and the more specific notion of a physical body (in Chapter 7). In order to do all this, we shall (at least temporarily)[2] have to introduce a fifth primitive notion, that of an experience.

The word 'experience' has several uses among philosophers and ordinary men. We might in ordinary parlance say that visiting India or seeing the Taj Mahal was an interesting experience; but in the narrow sense of 'experience' that I shall be using and that is, I believe, quite common among philosophers, such things do not count literally as experiences, even if they involve experiences. In my usage such things as someone's feeling (of) pain and someone's seeing (of) red are paradigms of experiences, or (what I take to be the same thing) of experiencings.

This notion of (an) experience, like the other notions we have been using as primitives, is not just an arbitrary primitive with which to attempt the definition of the concepts we wish to

[2] In Ch. 8, I shall try to define away the notions of experience and exact likeness, in terms of our three other primitive notion-clusters.

define. The notion of likeness has long been thought very basic, central, or (ontogenetically) primitive, so it seemed appropriate to use that notion, or at least the related less vague notion of exact alikeness, as a primitive in defining other notions in Chapter 2. Similarly, the notion of an experience is by no means an *historically* arbitrary notion to use as a primitive in defining or explicating the notion of a being or self. For many philosophers have tried to explain what it is to be a being or self in terms of some sort of ordering or arrangement of experiences (or sense data, or perceptions, etc).[3]

Of course, those philosophers who have explained the self in terms of some ordering of experiences, sense data, etc., have typically done so, I think, at least partly because they thought that (reasonable belief about) experience(s) was in some sense epistemologically basic, and in some sense epistemologically prior to (reasonable belief about) physical bodies and/or other minds. And there have been many arguments in recent years against the existence of any such kind of basicness or priority. Some of these arguments, e.g., those of Austin in *Sense and Sensibilia*,[4] have force against certain particular conceptions of the epistemological basicness or priority of experiences. But I believe that there is a definite sense, nonetheless, in which experience is basic and prior, a sense whose validity is not touched by any arguments I know of. In particular, I think that it is impossible for any statements about the external world or other minds to be reasonable ones for a certain being to believe at a certain time without there being any statements about experience that it is reasonable for that being to believe at that time, but that the reverse does not hold; and if that is so, there is a perfectly good sense in which experience is epistemologically prior and perhaps basic.[5] There is no time to go into the matter further here, but if what has just been said is

[3] E.g., Hume in the *Treatise*; and Ayer in *The Problem of Knowledge*.
[4] Oxford: Clarendon, 1962, Ch. 10.
[5] I have argued for this idea at greater length in the Introduction to *Reason and Scepticism*.

correct, then we have additional reason to use 'experience' as a primitive in a system of metaphysical definitions. After all, metaphysical and epistemological considerations are related, and in philosophy we want ultimately to integrate and systematically unify our ideas in epistemology and metaphysics. So if we are going to treat experience as in some sense epistemologically basic, there are reasons of systematic coherence and symmetry to use 'experience' as primitive basic building block in constructing definitions of important metaphysical notions. [6]

What I should like now to show is that there is an important ontological relation between experiences and (animate) beings who have them, of such a sort that one can go a long way towards defining the notion of a being (or self) in terms of that relation. The relation between experiences and beings is not, however, as simple as some philosophers have thought. Philosophers like Descartes and, perhaps, Hume have thought that a self or being essentially: exists only while it is having experiences or thinking. Locke argued against Descartes' position with the picturesque reminder that every drowsy nod shakes that position. [7] The point is that we do sometimes sleep dreamlessly, so that it would appear that a being can exist at a time when it has no experiences. Indeed, I think we can even make the stronger claim that a being can exist without *ever* having any experiences. An argument for the logical possibility and verifiability of the existence of such a being is given by P. Unger in 'On Experience and the Development of the Understanding'. [8] Unger discusses the possibility of having a machine for creating cell-by-cell duplicates of people; and he shows how one might knowingly create a being that never had any experiences, by

[6] There is a similar reason for using exact likeness as a metaphysical primitive here, if, as I argued in *Reason and Scepticism*, Ch. 5, that notion is involved in some of our most ultimate inductive standards or principles, and is thus basic to an epistemological understanding of our empirical thinking.

[7] *Essay Concerning Human Understanding*, Book II, Ch. 1.

[8] *Amer. Phil. Quarterly* 3, 1966, pp. 48–56.

duplicating a given person while he was in a dreamless sleep, letting the duplicate exist for a few minutes in the same kind of dreamless sleep, and then destroying the duplicate before it (or he or she) ever awakened or had any dreams.

In the light of such cases, it would seem that any attempt to define what it is to be a being in terms of actually existing experiences is bound to fail. How, then, is one to state a relation between beings and experiences that *is* analytic of beinghood or selfhood? Perhaps by talking not of *actual* experiences, but only of the experiences a conscious being *could* or *might* have. I may well be logically capable of existing without experiences, but if I have certain experiences, they will logically depend on me, will essentially exist only when I do.

I want to claim, therefore, that even if beings are at most accidentally: existent only if at some time possessed of experiences, the experiences that a being may have can be logically dependent on that being. Thus we can say that:

(a) of necessity anything $x$ is a being or self only if $x$ is an entity that can exist at one time and not another (and so is contingent), that is not itself a change, and that can alter,[9] such that it is logically possible for there to be an experience that logically depends on $x$.[10]

This relation between (possible) experiences and beings is, I believe, analytic of what it is to be a being, and if so, then the notion of a being is at least in part definable by essence and accident, since the notion of (logical) dependence involves the notion of essence. We said earlier that it is possible for a self or being to exist without ever having experiences. For similar

[9] This first part of (a) rules out platonic entities (like propositions), facts about selves, worms of selves, logicians' sets of selves, and changes of selves from counting as selves, or beings.

[10] Our talk of logical dependence by experiences on beings eliminates the need to talk of beings *having* experiences, and so obviates the need for an additional primitive notion of having.

reasons I think it is *impossible* for there to be a self or being that essentially exists only if at some time possessed of some experience. And we can add this claim to our statement of the conditions analytic of beinghood, by adding to what we have said in condition (a) that:

(b) of necessity any $x$ is a being or self only if $x$ is not essentially: existent only if at some time when $x$ exists, an experience exists.

Condition (b) is needed in our definition of beinghood, because there are putative entities other than beings or selves that meet condition (a) but fail condition (b). This is true, for example, of particular experiences, since they depend on themselves but are essentially experiences, and thus essentially exist only if at some time when they exist, an experience exists. Consider too the kind or species experience. The species or kind mankind is, if it exists, an entity that essentially exists just when some man exists; and the species experience is, if it exists at all, an entity that essentially: exists just when some experience exists. It follows that it is possible for experiences to depend on the species experience, assuming only that certain experiences are or would be essentially experiences. And in that case the species experience meets condition (a). But it is in any case ruled out by (b), for obvious reasons.[11] (In speaking of species, kinds, or classes here, I am using those terms in something like the way biologists do, and am not referring to logicians' sets or classes. My assumption that species are not ontologically just like sets will

---

[11] (b) rules out duos, trios, etc., of experiences, and also subclasses or subspecies of experiences. But (b) does not eliminate such 'queer' entities as: my experiencing pain or being able to speak Russian. In order for our definition to proceed successfully, such entities should be eliminated at this point. There are certain ways of complicating conditions (a) and (b) that would, I think, enable us to eliminate them, but I shall not go into the details here, except to say that such elimination may, e.g., be feasible with the help of the *negation* of the condition (d) described on page 128f., below.

be justified in Chapter 5, below, but in any case that assumption makes things harder, not easier, for us in the present chapter.) It would seem, then, that we need to use both (a) and (b) in stating the necessary and sufficient conditions of beinghood, in defining the notion of a being by essence and accident.[12]


## II


I would like now to consider whether (a) and (b) are sufficient for the definition of beinghood, or rather just constitute necessary conditions of beinghood. To discern the answer to this question, we should look around to see whether there are any (putative) abstract or concrete entities that are ontologically related to, but not identical with, beings and that meet conditions (a) and (b). If we can think of such (putative) entities, we shall have to add to our definition of beinghood.

Conditions (a) and (b) do rule out such being-related entities as groups and assemblages of beings, and social institutions. For it would seem that any experiences of members of or participants in a group, assemblage, or institution would be logically capable of surviving the dispersal or destruction of the group, assemblage, or institution, and in that case groups, assemblages and institutions fail condition (a) as stated above. Consider, however, the species (or class or kind) human being.

---

[12] Actually, (a) is not an entirely uncontroversial necessary condition of beinghood. Hume in the *Treatise* thought that experiences, or at least impressions, might not depend on any self and might exist 'unowned'. And in *The Problem of Knowledge*, p. 197, Ayer somewhat more plausibly holds that even though experiences have to be owned, they do not depend on their owners and could have been owned by someone else. But to suggest that a certain experience (experiencing), say, of pain on my part could have been had or done by someone else is like saying that the fall (falling) I take or do at some time could have been taken or done by another person. And I really do not know how to make sense of such an idea. Thus my assumption of (a).

It would appear that I am only accidentally always a human being, so I do not logically depend on the human race. Thus even if a given experience depends on me, a human, it will not depend on the species mankind, if it can continue to exist when I am turned into something non-human and all other humans perish. But even if humans are not essentially humans, they are essentially: existent only while there are (animate) beings or selves. The class or species or race of beings will thus be depended on by any experience that depends on some human or other being, since given beings seem to depend on the species or race of beings. Since this class or species or race of beings is neither immutable nor itself a change, and since it no more essentially exists only if there are experiences at some time when it exists, than I do, it meets (a) and (b) without counting as a being. So (a) and (b) are insufficient for the definition of what it is to be a being or self.

There are in fact other races, kinds, species or classes (in other than the logicians' sense of 'class') that meet (a) and (b) without being animate beings. Consider, for example, the class of things identical with Johnson or with Nixon.[13] Any experience of Nixon that depends on Nixon will also depend on that class, since Nixon depends on that class. Nixon couldn't exist when the class of things identical with Johnson *or* Nixon did not. It should be clear, upon close examination, that this class meets (a) and (b).

Pairs and trios, etc., of beings are not species or classes of beings. A pair (or duo) exists only when both its members do, whereas species exist precisely as long as they have a single member. But duos are further examples of (putative or possible)

[13] It is odd to call such things as these classes (in the biological, as opposed to the logicians' sense, of the term); but such talk about *classes* can be eliminated in favour of talk about certain *states of affairs*. We can talk about there being something identical with either Johnson or Nixon, rather than about the class of (things identical with either) Johnson or Nixon. And we can, e.g., talk about there being experiences, rather than about the class (or species) of experiences. Cf. Ch. 5, below, for more explanation of this.

entities that meet (a) and (b) but are not beings. The pair
Nixon and Johnson is, for example, logically depended on by
such cross-personal or joint experiencings as Nixon's feeling
pain while Johnson feels sad, since such experiencings can exist
only when both Nixon and Johnson do, and thus only when the
pair Nixon and Johnson exists.[14] Similarly for trios, quartets,
etc., of selves or beings.

Consider, finally, certain mental dispositions or abilities that
meet (a) and (b) but are clearly not beings. Perhaps no experience
depends on my ability to speak French or play the clarinet, but
experiences will, I think, depend on my ability to have experiences. So such abilities probably are not ruled out by (a) and
(b). Consider too that if experiences can depend on particular
mental abilities, they can depend on the class or species of such
abilities, since, presumably, every mental ability is essentially a
mental ability. So that class or species also seems to meet (a)
and (b). Thus any conditions we add to (a) and (b) in order to
define beinghood by essence and accident must take into account
and eliminate a large variety of entities that (may exist and)
meet (a) and (b), but are not conscious beings, entities of all the
various sorts we have just been discussing.

Let us call any (possible or putative) entity that meets (a) and
(b) a cobrace—short for 'conscious being or race of conscious
beings', but since things other than beings or races of them can
be cobraces, this explanation is strictly mnemonic. We have in
effect been saying that of necessity only cobraces are beings, and
that this is analytic of beinghood. But what else is analytically
necessary to beinghood? What *kind* of cobrace does something
have to be in order to count as a being? If we can define being-

---

[14] I am not disallowing joint experiences as experiences, for if I did, my
definition of beinghood might be accused of circularity on the grounds
that it was based implicitly on the notion of an experience *of a single being*.
Also, I am assuming that pairs exist independently of how closely their
members are related. If this is mistaken, we can always talk of the state of
affairs consisting in both Nixon and Johnson existing, rather than of the
pair Nixon and Johnson.

hood or selfhood in terms of the notion of a cobrace and the primitives we have been using, then since the notion of a cobrace has been defined via those primitives, we will have furnished a definition by essence and accident of beinghood or selfhood constructed by means of our five primitive notions or notion-clusters.

We can perhaps best see how to provide such a definition if we examine some of the relations of ontological dependence among various cobraces. Note, for example, the following important difference between beings and the race or species or class of beings. Beings do not depend on other beings, but do depend on the race of beings; the latter, however, depends on no particular being. Furthermore, the race of beings is essentially such as to be logically depended on by some being, and thus by some cobrace other than itself. It could not exist at a time when no beings existed, and of necessity every being depends on the race of beings. It is not, however, essential to any given being that there be some (other) cobrace dependent on it. There are *in fact* many cobraces that depend on Nixon, e.g., Nixon's ability to have experiences, the pair Nixon and Johnson, the trio Nixon, Johnson, and Humphrey, etc.[15] But Nixon is not essentially (such as to be) depended on by such entities. Nixon could exist if there were no Johnson, and thus no pair Nixon and Johnson that depended on him. And I think Nixon could even exist without having the power or ability to have experiences. Consider the case of an enchanted prince in a dreamless sleep. Surely it is a being or self that is asleep, though the prince is in some sense, or metaphorically speaking, a 'living vegetable'. Yet the prince's enchantment may deprive him of the power to dream or be awake. It is logically possible for Nixon to be enchanted in this way and still exist in a sleeping

---

[15] I assume that such entities as pairs and abilities exist. Even if they do not, we have no overwhelming argument to show that this is so, and so I am taking such entities into account in my definitions. Again, this makes things harder, not easier, for me. On this subject, see the Introduction, p. 3f., above.

state (until the spell is broken). So it would seem that Nixon is not essentially: depended on by his ability to have experiences, since he could exist without that ability. And if Nixon and other beings are not essentially: depended on by mental abilities of this sort, neither are they essentially: depended on by the class or species of mental abilities. Even if Nixon could not exist in the absence of the class of mental abilities—which itself is not entirely clear—still the class of mental abilities could never *depend* on Nixon or on any other given being. Such classes require for their existence only that there be *some contemporaneous being or other* with mental abilities.

I think then that:

(c) of necessity any $x$ is a being or self only if $x$ is a cobrace that is at most accidentally (such as to be) logically depended on by some cobrace other than $x$.

Condition (c), we have seen, is not met by the race or class of beings, and so the latter can now be eliminated. (c) also eliminates such races or classes as the class of things identical with Nixon or Johnson. For that class or race cannot exist unless either Nixon or Johnson does, and both Nixon and Johnson must be cobraces that depend on but are not identical with that class or race. So that class or race essentially: exists only if some other cobrace depends on it, and thus fails condition (c). Similarly, for the class of Johnson, Nixon, or Humphrey, and other such classes or races.

However, (c) does not eliminate certain other sorts of cobraces that we need to eliminate before we have a sufficient definition of beinghood. The duo Nixon and Johnson depends on Nixon, even though Nixon does not depend on it. In fact the trio Nixon, Johnson, and Humphrey depends on that duo; but the duo does not depend on the trio, since it could exist even when Humphrey, and thus the trio, did not. The duo is only accidentally depended on by the trio. So it seems that the duo Nixon and Johnson meets condition (c) even though it is not a being or self. We need another condition of selfhood in order to eliminate these and other non-selves and provide an adequate definition of selfhood or beinghood.

This can, I think, be done as follows. Let us define independent cobraces as cobraces that meet the conditions stated in (c). Beings count as independent cobraces, and so, we have seen, do various duos (pairs) and trios, etc., of beings. I shall also assume that certain mental abilities that are cobraces, e.g., my ability to experience, are also independent cobraces.[16] But what about the class or species of mental abilities? Is this cobrace an independent cobrace? The answer to this question depends on whether selves can exist not only without the ability to have experiences, but totally devoid of any mental abilities. If it *is* possible for there to be a being or self without any mental abilities—an idiot or a baby, for example—then I think the class of mental abilities does count as an independent cobrace. If it is *not* possible, then it is not an independent cobrace, for then necessarily any given being will depend on the class of mental abilities (where such a class is, of course, understood as existing in the manner of a species). But then since the class of mental abilities essentially exists only when there are beings, it essentially exists only if *depended on* by beings, and so, only if depended on by cobraces other than itself. Thus if it is not possible for a self or being to lack all mental abilities, we can eliminate the class of mental abilities by condition (c). But if it is possible, then we again need some other condition to eliminate that class, in order to define the concept of a being.

I think that a single further condition (d) will serve to distinguish beings from all the various other possible entities that we have not, or *may* not have, yet eliminated via condition (c),

---

[16] This assumption is dubious, but making it only makes things harder. Note that such entities as the species or class of visual-experiences-or-red-things meet (a) and (b), but fail (c), because they of necessity are depended on by some more 'specific' class or other that is a cobrace, e.g., the class of colored-visual-experiences-or-red-things. This is also why my ability to experience probably fails condition (c).

or thus via any of our conditions of beinghood, since (c) entails (a) and (b).

(d) of necessity anything $x$ is a being or self *if and only if $x$ is* an independent cobrace that is at most accidentally: existent at some time $t$ only if some independent cobrace not identical with $x$ exists at $t$.

This condition (d), which entails condition (c) but is a good deal stronger, can be seen to separate beings from other possible independent cobraces as follows.

Duos and trios, etc., essentially exist only if they have members. So duos and trios of beings essentially exist only if and when there are other independent cobraces, namely, particular beings, and thus fail (d). Next consider various mental abilities like my ability to have experiences. Such an ability essentially exists only when I do, and thus only when some other independent cobrace exists. So such abilities also fail (d). Finally, the class of mental abilities is essentially existent only when some being exists, and thus again, only when some other independent cobrace exists. So it too fails (d).

What about beings or selves? In the first place, beings are at most accidentally: existent only if and when there are other beings. Therefore, beings are at most accidentally: existent only when duos, etc., of beings exist. Nor, as we saw above, is any being essentially: existent only when its ability to have experiences, or some similar cobrace mental ability, exists. Enchanted (or comatose) princes are possible. Nor, finally, do beings essentially exist only when the class or species of mental abilities exists, assuming that beings can exist without mental abilities. If so, then it would seem that beings *do* meet condition (d), and, further, that only beings meet that condition.

I have, of course, just assumed that a being can exist without any mental abilities. But if this is not possible, it will still be true that beings and only beings meet (d). For in that case, the class of mental abilities will be essentially: depended on by selves, but *will not count as an independent cobrace*, so that it will still be the case that beings can exist even when no other independent cobraces exist, and thus that beings meet condition (d). Thus (d) seems to formulate logically necessary and sufficient conditions for something to count as an (animate or conscious) being or a self.[17] And in that case we can offer as our final definition of beinghood:

*⌜a is a being (or self)⌝ has approximately the same meaning

[17] If beings depend on (parts of) their brains, then (parts of) brains will be cobraces and need to be eliminated if our definition of beinghood is to work, because brains are not beings, at least if one's brain can outlast oneself. In such a case, it is or would be necessary to add to our definition. Since, as far as I can tell, (parts of) brains may meet condition (c) and count as independent cobraces, it may be necessary to add to our definition a condition to the effect that (c′) of necessity anything $x$ is a being only if $x$ essentially depends on an independent cobrace that can at some time fail to be everywhere $x$ is. If people depend on brain parts, then they (essentially) depend on independent cobraces that can fail to be located at every place where they (the people) are located. For, as I shall argue in the next chapter, a person's body is not exterior to him; and a person's body can be located in places where his brain is not. So selves meet (c′), if people and other beings depend on (parts of) their brains. But (parts of) brains themselves do not meet (c′), because (as I shall argue in Chapter 7, below) they do not depend on *their* parts, and because even though they depend on matter (in general), matter, for various reasons, fails condition (c) and is not an independent cobrace. Thus (c′) can be used to eliminate brain parts, if necessary; and if (c′) is used, we can call entities meeting (a), (b), (c) and (c′) very independent cobraces and complete our definitional conditions of beinghood with a condition (d′) that is like our present (d) except for having 'very independent cobrace' wherever (d) has 'independent cobrace'. I shall argue below for the logical possibility of (our) disembodied existence. If such disembodiment is possible or if it is possible to exchange one's whole brain for another and still exist, then (c′) is unnecessary, and our definition can remain as it is in the body of the text. Whether (c′) is needed depends on the debatable issue of the conceptual coherence of brain interchange, etc. Until this issue is cleared up, we will not be entirely clear about what is involved in being a being, and thus about the concept of a being. Hence my hesitation between two possible definitions of beinghood. Defining a concept about which there exist difficult *conceptual* issues may be as hard as resolving those conceptual issues.

as ⌜there is an $x$ identical with $a$ such that $x$ is an independent cobrace that is at most accidentally: existent at some time $t$ only if some independent cobrace not identical with $x$ exists at $t$⌝.

We have thus fulfilled our promise to construct a definition by essence and accident of the notion of a being or self by means of our five primitive notion-clusters.

In common parlance (as opposed to *some* philosophical discourse), plants and rocks and numbers do not count as beings,[18] but enchanted, unintelligent, comatose or disembodied creatures do count as beings. I think we have defined this metaphysically important ordinary notion of a being. We may not, on the other hand, have defined the notion of a self, if, as some people would argue, an experiencing being that lacks self-consciousness does not count as a self. And for similar reasons our definition would not, perhaps, be adequate to define the notion of a subject. Perhaps we have also failed to provide conditions that define the notions of an animate being or a conscious being. Animateness may involve biological aliveness; and something may have to be at least capable of consciousness (and not enchanted or comatose) to count as a conscious being. And our definition of beinghood does nothing to insure these further conditions. It should be noted, finally, that our definition is clearly insufficient to define the notion of a person, which is narrower than that of a being. But if we have succeeded at least in defining the very general notion of a being, then I think our efforts in this chapter have by no means been in vain.

[18] This is pointed out by Fowler, *op. cit.*, p. 141 (article on 'entity').

# 4. Conscious Beings and the Physical

It is time now to consider the relation between (conscious or animate) beings or selves and physical entities generally. I shall be arguing that conscious beings, and mental or psychical entities generally, are never identical with any physical entities, and shall try to show that it is possible to define the notion of a physical entity by contrast with the notion of a being or self.

## I

Everybody knows that there are contingently true identity *statements* or *propositions*. But it has long seemed to many philosophers and modal logicians that if one allows quantification into modal contexts (and so accepts the meaningfulness of Essentialism) and if one accepts an appropriate version of Leibniz's Law of the Indiscernibility of Identicals, one cannot hold that there are any contingently identical *entities*. For consider any identical $x$ and $y$. The latter clearly will be (have the modal property of being) necessarily: existent only if and when (it is) identical with $y$. So by Leibniz's Law, the former will have that property too. So for any $x$ and $y$, $x$ will be identical with $y$, only if $x$ is necessarily: existent only if and when (it is) identical with $y$, and thus only if it is necessary that: $x$ is identical with $y$ if and when $x$ exists.[1] It would appear, then, that there is an important sense in which, speaking *de re*, we can correctly say that entities are never contingently identical. From

[1] This kind of argument occurs in, among other places, Kripke's 'Identity and Necessity'.

this it pretty clearly follows, furthermore, that identical $x$ and $y$ will logically depend on one another, will be mutually logically dependent. For if $x$ has to be identical with $y$, when it exists, then it cannot exist when $y$ does not, and so depends on $y$; and similarly if $y$ has to be identical with $x$ when it exists. And we already know that if $x$ and $y$ are identical, then $x$ *will* have to be identical with $y$ when it exists and $y$ *will* have to be identical with $x$ when it exists.

On the basis of these facts about identity, I think there is definite reason to favour dualism as a theory of the relation of mind and body. For if I and other actual beings are only accidentally always embodied, only accidentally never become disembodied, then we do not *logically depend* on our bodies or, presumably, on any other physical entities. And in that case it would seem that we are not identical with anything physical, and that dualism is true. The fact that we seem to be able to imagine in some detail what it would be like to become disembodied is, I think, prima facie evidence that such disembodiment is logically possible.[2] Unless there is some philosophically plausible argument against the possibility of our disembodiment, we have definite reason—on the basis of imagination—to think that our disembodiment is logically possible and that dualism is true.

Of course, there have been many arguments put forward against the logical possibility of (our) disembodiment. Some of these assume some kind of Verificationism and are weak not only because of the weakness of the various principles of verifiability that have been proposed, but because of the seeming abundance of possible situations in which evidence for and reason to believe in disembodied existence (on our part) would exist.[3]

---

[2] For imaginative description of disembodiment, see Ayer, *The Problem of Knowledge*, p. 193, and Strawson, *Individuals*, London: Methuen, 1959, p. 115f. For more on the evidential relationship between imagination and logical possibility, see *Reason and Scepticism*, pp. 54ff.

[3] For description of some such situations, see *Reason and Scepticism*, Ch. 1, sect. 1.

Some philosophers would argue against dualism on the grounds that even though it is possible in principle for beings to become disembodied, such a thing is not possible for beings who are embodied the way we are. We, at least, the argument goes, are too intimately connected with our bodies to become unembodied. It is hard to know what to say against this position. But it does seem to me much more plausible, on the face of it, to deny the possibility of disembodiment in general, than to say that disembodiment is possible for some possible creatures but not for us, the way this position does. Consider, in particular, the disembodied state of those possible creatures who supposedly could become disembodied. Can they not be thinking and imagining and willing in such a state? But if we with our thinking, etc., are not capable of disembodiment, then presumably our thinking, etc., is not qualitatively just like the thinking, etc., of those possible disembodied creatures. For it is hard to understand how creatures with thoughts, etc., *just like ours* could be disembodied while *we* were logically *incapable* of having such thoughts in a disembodied state. But then if the position we are examining takes refuge in the claim that disembodied beings would have thoughts, imaginings, etc., that were qualitatively quite unlike our own, it runs the risk of unintelligibility. For do we really have any kind of clear or intuitive understanding of what imaginative experience or thinking quite unlike our own would be? In addition, even assuming that such creatures would have thoughts, imaginings, etc., unlike all our own present thoughts, imaginings, etc., we have seen no reason to think that we could not become disembodied and start having thoughts, imaginings, etc., of the kind disembodied creatures would have, but we do not have. So I do not think it is possible to undermine dualism along these lines.

Another argument against dualism rests on the difficulty of reconciling the logical possibility of our disembodiment with the fact that we essentially originate in or derive from (certain) matter.[4] It is hard to see how we could essentially come from

[4] Cf. Kripke, 'Naming and Necessity', footnote 77.

matter and yet only accidentally continue to be connected with matter. Perhaps this difficulty will seem less worrisome, however, if we recall the above-argued-for thesis that the past places greater (logical) restrictions on individuals than does the future. In the light of our earlier distinction between past and future, it is perhaps not so implausible to say that the past of an individual could be tied to (certain) matter, even though his future was not. An analogy may be helpful here. Just as the Ford Motor Company is essentially founded by Henry Ford, but can exist after the latter, and his descendants, cease to exist; so too we may be essentially derived from or 'founded by' (certain) matter and yet capable (logically or metaphysically) of existing without matter. The challenge to dualism from this quarter is not, I think, overwhelming.

It might, however, be thought that I have made my case for dualism rest too heavily on the possibility of (our) disembodiment. After all, it could be said, even if disembodied existence is impossible, various mental states and processes may still fail to depend and be depended on by the kinds of physical (brain) states and processes with which mind-body identity theorists have sought to identify them. It might be argued, in particular, that since my being in pain (or any particular pain of mine)[5] is not logically depended on by any brain state or process like c-fibre stimulation in my brain (since there can be instances of such stimulation without the state of my being in pain or any pains or other mental phenomena existing anywhere), my being in pain (or any particular pain of mine) is not identical with any given brain state or process, and dualism is thus true. But this would be mistaken. All that follows from the fact that my pains and my being in pain are not depended on by such brain states or processes as c-fibre stimulation is that such mental entities

---

[5] On the kind of identity theory held, e.g., by D. M. Armstrong (in *A Materialist Theory of the Mind*, London: 1968), certain physical entities function as pains and are both identical and mutually logically dependent with pains. But such a view involves claiming that pains are not essentially mental or psychical, and is thus intuitively implausible, I think.

are not identical with those non-mental physical entities with which mind-body identity theorists have attempted to identify them and with which they are supposed to be empirically correlated. But that does not prevent one from saying that pains and my being in pain are themselves physical states of or processes in my body or brain, because they logically depend on my body or brain. In other words, if states like c-fibre stimulation in my brain count as physical because of their dependence on (there being) physical bodies, one could say that various *mental* states or processes are *also physical*, because dependent on (there being) bodies, even if they are not identical with any *non-mental* physical states or processes like c-fibre stimulation. And it might be reasonable to say that even selves were physical states or aspects of physical bodies, if they depended on such bodies and could not become disembodied. Such a view may be incompatible with contingent mind-body identity theory à la Feigl and Smart, but we should probably also not call such a view dualism, since it clearly does not hold there to be any separation between the mental and physical realms, does not say there are mental or psychical entities that are *not* physical. To have clear-cut reason to hold that mental states and processes are not physical, one would need to have reason to think of such entities as independent of the physical the way c-fibre stimulation is not, and so, presumably, reason to believe in the possibility of our disembodiment. That is why I have made our argument for dualism depend on that latter possibility.

Of course, if it turns out that disembodied survival is impossible for beings in the actual world, the view we have just been discussing may well be true, and more reasonably believed to be true than traditional mind-body identity theory. The latter mistakenly argues from the existence of contingently true identity statements to the conclusion that mental and physical entities are contingently identical. But there is no contingent identity between entities; and, moreover, mental states like my being in pain are not (logically) depended on by the physical states or processes like c-fibre stimulation in my brain with which they are supposed to be correlated, as even most mind-body identity theorists are willing to grant. Given a proper understanding of entity-identity, then, particular mental states are not identical with the particular brain or bodily states with which mind-body identity theorists have sought to identify them, and mind-body identity theory seems simply to be mistaken. And inasmuch, furthermore, as we have been given no reason to deny the logical possibility of our disembodiment, our imagination gives us some reason to maintain that we *could* become disembodied, and thus to maintain a form of dualism.[6]

## II

By means of the conclusions argued for above about the merely contingent relations between mental and physical entities, we can, I think, frame a definition by essence and accident of what it is for an entity to be physical. We have tentatively argued that selves require nothing physical for their existence. But then it is not implausible to claim that selves or beings are not physical. That is not to say that beings are not partly physical or that they lack a physical aspect or 'side' to them. Indeed, I shall be arguing below that one's body is in no way exterior or merely attached to one, so that it may be in order to say that various beings are partly, or in one aspect, physical. But it does not follow that such beings are physical *simpliciter*. Consider a parallel. If there is a table that is mostly metal, but also partly wooden, then if we separate those two parts with a minimum of alteration to either and then destroy the wooden part, we may have the right to say that the table still exists. But this will not be so if, instead, we completely destroy the metal part of the table. And for that reason, I think, we may say that the original table was partly wooden and partly metal, but cannot correctly say that the table

---

[6] Similar arguments against the identity theory and for dualism occur in *Reason and Scepticism* and in the earlier-mentioned papers of Kripke.

was originally wooden *simpliciter*—even if we can, perhaps, say that the table was originally metal *simpliciter*.

Now if we can at all reasonably think of a given being or person as having within him, or not exterior to him, two aspects, parts, or elements—namely, a psyche or personality and a body —and if a being can survive the total destruction of his body, then I think we have as much reason to say that such a being is at most partly physical, and not physical *simpliciter*, as we had to say of the table described above that it was at most partly wooden.

If we say that selves or beings are not physical entities, then I think we should probably also say that all entities that depend on (there being) selves or experiences are not physical *simpliciter*. And we can, I think, even say that all (possible) entities that essentially: exist only if some being or experience exists at some time or other, are not physical *simpliciter*. Furthermore, given dualism, I think that anything a self or its experiences could depend on would necessarily fail to be physical itself;[7] and the same for anything that essentially: exists if there ever are any selves or experiences. I would like to conclude, then, that:

(a) of necessity any $x$ is (a) physical (entity) only if $x$ is at most accidentally existent only if some self exists at some time; and only if $x$ is essentially not depended on by any self, or experience, and is not essentially: existent if there ever is an experience.

Condition (a) does not rule out lakes, flowers, or soil-erosion as physical, but does deny that status to beings, races or kinds of beings, space-time worms of beings, facts about beings, pairs of beings, and various of the other kinds of entities associated with selves that we mentioned in Chapter 3. (a) also eliminates from physical status any and all necessary entities—e.g., universals or propositions—that may exist. But (a) is only necessary,

---

[7] I *assume* here that if selves are disembodiable, all their experiences (in our undefined sense of the term) are also disembodiable.

not sufficient, for the definition of physicalness, because there are things that are not physical that it fails to rule out as such. Take, for example, the race, or class, of entities-existing-while-there-are-no-mental-entities. Such an entity would meet (a), but does not seem to be physical. Its existence, for example, does not appear to require that there be any physical bodies or matter in the universe. Such an entity can, however, be eliminated if we claim that:

(b) of necessity any $x$ is physical only if $x$ does not essentially: exist at every time when something exists but no beings exist.

Conditions (a) and (b) may not themselves suffice to define physicalness. Space, Time, parts of space, moments of time, etc., all may meet (a) and (b) and yet may not count as physical entities. Such entities could be ruled out, if we wanted, by adding to our conditions of physicalness that:

(c) of necessity any $x$ is physical only if $x$ is located in space, and can be located in some places but not others,[8] but is not identical with Space or Time, any part or interval of Space or Time, any point or moment of Space or Time, etc.

With the addition of (c), I think we have come close to conditions that are individually necessary and jointly sufficient for physicalness, and so are close to being able to give a plausible definition by essence and accident of what it is to be physical, using only our five primitive notion-clusters.[9] However, there remain

[8] This phrase is added to eliminate facts about physical entities. Such facts may be located in Space in general, but they cannot be located in some places as opposed to others, I think. More on the nature of facts in Ch. 6, below, where, I hope, it will become clear why we should not want to call facts about the physical physical entities themselves.

[9] Even if hunger feelings are in some sense physical because of their physical causality or because they are phenomenologically 'of' the physical, there may still be a sense in which physicalness is an ontological status lacked by hunger feelings; this is the sense of the term I mean to define.

certain possible counterexamples to any definition of physicalness in terms of (a), (b), and (c) *alone*. We shall consider these counterexamples only later, in Chapter 5 (p. 83n.), when we shall be in a better position to handle them and really complete our definition of physicalness. In any case, there are certain possible objections to our use of condition (a) in defining the physical, and these objections should be considered before we proceed any further.

For one thing, if dualism is false then, as I argued above, beings and their experiences may well be physical; and in that case, (a) will not formulate a necessary condition of physicalness, so that any definition of physicalness based on (a) will be in error. Since I do not think we can be sure that disembodied existence is logically or metaphysically possible, or that dualism is true, I think it must be admitted that our proposed (preliminary) definition of the physical based on (a), (b), and (possibly) (c) may be mistaken. But even if dualism is false, it will still, I think, be possible to define physicalness by essence and accident. For we will be able to say that:

of necessity any $x$ is (a) physical (entity) if and only if $x$ is a contingent entity that is at most accidentally not located in some places but not others,

perhaps adding that $x$ is not a part of Space or locus of points in Space, etc. To the extent that the question of disembodiment, and thus of dualism, is a conceptual question of great difficulty, it is at present impossible to decide which of the two possible ways of going about defining physicalness that we have mentioned is correct, with any confidence. But the same reasons that incline me towards dualism also incline me at least to favour the use of conditions (a), (b) and (possibly) (c) in defining the physical.

It might be objected to our definition of the physical in terms of (a), (b), and (c) that even if those conditions bring to light certain modal properties that *for a priori reasons* and *of necessity* are possessed by all and only physical entities,[10] it does not follow, and there is no reason to believe, that those conditions can be used to give an *analytic definition* of the notion of physicalness. (Similar objections may have occurred to the reader concerning our definitions of future and past, or others of the definitions offered earlier.) However, other things being equal, apriority and necessity is most readily and best explained in terms of the analyticity of what is a priori and necessary. And given our desire for a definition of physicalness (or other concepts we have attempted to define), and the lack of equally plausible and conceptually parsimonious alternative definitions of physicalness (or those other concepts), we have reason to think of what we have said about physicalness (or those other concepts) as analytic and definitive thereof—at least until we find counterexamples to things we have said or can find some really specific strong argument against thinking of what we have been doing as definition.

At this point, however, the critic of our definition of the physical might object to our using condition (a) to define physicalness by contrast with the mental or psychical realm. Surely, the objection goes, the physical can and should be understood independently of the mental. But why think that this is so? Perhaps, because one would ideally like to be able to define the physical and mental realms independently of one another and from one's definition (and other information) deduce the answers to questions about the ontological relations between the mental and the physical. Perhaps, one would like, ideally, to do this, but my own feeling is that unless we bring in some new undefined term(s), we cannot define the physical without contrasting it with the mental or psychical. More significantly, furthermore, there are, as far as I can tell, no available half-way plausible definitions of the physical that avoid con-

[10] Of course, particular essentialistic claims about the physical may be necessary and *empirical* (cf. Kripke, *op. cit.*). It may be a priori that physical things have a certain property $p$ essentially, but a posteriori that *Old Smoky* has $p$ essentially (or is physical).

trasting it with the mental, so I think we have some justification
for defining physicalness as we have.

Actually, I think one can go further and argue that there are
positive reasons for wanting to define the physical by contrast
with the mental. For the idea that we can only understand the
physical or the material as what is *not* mental (but exists contingently, etc.) is not without its philosophical antecedents.
Moore held that the notion of a physical or material object was
to be defined in terms of the fact that material objects are not
sense data, nor minds, nor acts of consciousness.[11] And W.
Kneale has argued that 'matter has always been distinguished
by exclusion. . . . In the physical science which has flourished
since the seventeenth century it is contrasted primarily with
mind and everything that depends essentially upon mind. . . .'[12]

I think that understanding and defining the notion of physicalness by contrast with the notion of mentalness or psychicness
is no mere stop-gap in the absence of a better way to define
physicalness, but is, in fact, on the right track. As I said earlier,
I am inclined to think that belief about experience is epistemologically prior to belief in the external world or other minds.
Our ultimate justification for the latter kinds of belief depends
in part, I think, on our having reasonable beliefs about experience. If so, then it becomes somewhat plausible (and there are
reasons of philosophical system and symmetry) to hold that the
notion of the physical can be defined in terms of and by contrast with the notion of an experience (or of a being that can
have experiences)—just as our definition of the physical, of
physicalness, attempts to do. For if we have reason to believe
in a physical realm existing independently of us and our
experience only if we have reasonable beliefs about ourselves
and our experiences, then perhaps we can only understand the
physical as that which in the appropriate way is logically

[11] *Some Main Problems of Philosophy*, London: Allen and Unwin, 1953,
p. 131.

[12] Review of D. M. Armstrong, *A Materialist Theory of the Mind*, *Mind*
78, 1969, p. 300.

independent of us and our experiences, and so by contrast with our experiences and ourselves. And since we think of the physical as that which is there independently of whether *we* are there to perceive or be affected by it, as that which is fundamentally and unalterably different from *our experiencing* of it, perhaps these thoughts are built into our very concept of the physical in the way our definition suggests. Let us then at least tentatively assume the correctness of giving a contrast-definition by essence and accident of the notion of the physical.

## III

In assuming that there is a gulf between physical entities and beings and their experiences, we have in effect been assuming that of necessity beings are essentially not physical entities. But is it not logically possible for something physical to become (exist later as) a conscious being? Would it not be possible, for example, for a physical steam engine to develop into the kind of steam engine, like the Little Engine that Could, that could think, experience, and feel? And if such a thing happened, would we not have a being that was only accidentally not a physical entity and that only accidentally existed in a world where there were beings or selves? If such a case is possible, physical entities are not as greatly separated from beings or selves as we have assumed.

However, this objection rests on a confusion. Imagine the Little Engine that Could, for example, as actually existent. If it does exist, it is a being with hopes, feelings, thoughts, etc. Presumably, this being uses its wheels, etc., to do things, just as we use our arms, etc., to do things. So it would seem that we can contrast the Little Engine with its physical engine body if we can contrast ourselves with our bodies. If we, who think and feel, could become disembodied, why couldn't a being with a metal body do the same thing? And if the Little Engine does not depend on its body, it is not identical with that body. Now if a physical steam engine of the kind that actually exists in the world were gradually to alter in such a way that a being like the Little Engine that Could developed within it, then presumably the physical steam engine that existed before that development would still exist thereafter. After all, even after we have a steam-engine self present, there is still a physical metal engine present, and it is presumably the same one that was there before there was an engine self. Since, as we have seen, the engine self cannot be identical with its body, with the purely physical engine that is its body, we can conclude that the engine self is not identical with the physical steam engine that was originally present. And so the original physical engine has not become (does not exist later as) a conscious being or self with an engine body, a being like the Little Engine that Could. We still have no counter-example to the claim that of necessity beings or selves are essentially not physical entities and essentially exist only when beings (and thus the class or species of beings) exist.

'The engine' is generally used by us to refer to purely physical engines. But the Little Engine that Could of the children's story is a conscious being to whom the phrase 'the engine' is naturally used to refer. Thus phrases like 'the engine' or 'the tree' or 'the piano' can be used with two senses, or in two ways, in one of which they purport to refer to beings with engine, tree or piano bodies, and in the other of which they purport to refer to purely physical engines, trees, or pianos.

Something like this kind of ambiguity may, in fact, be responsible for certain possible further objections to the views we have been defending. Consider the fact, for example, that in *Oklahoma*, poor Judd, after he dies, is said to be lying serenely in his coffin. Similarly, a gravestone may say: here lies Joseph Green. But if Judd is lying in his coffin and Joseph Green lies under a gravestone, how can it be that these people no longer exist after they die, as has been held by philosophers who do not believe in an afterlife? And if Judd or Joseph Green is no longer a being or self right after he dies, but just a physical body, a corpse, then while he is a being and alive, he is not essentially not physical and is not essentially existent only when selves (and thus the species of selves) exist. And all this is incompatible with things we have said.

I think we can plausibly explain how we can say, e.g., that Judd is in his coffin and yet also say that Judd, the person, no longer exists, by claiming that referring expressions like 'Judd' can be used to refer either to a given entity or to what is left of, the remains of, that entity. Thus if I burn your antique desk to ashes, and you come and ask me where the desk is, I could say 'there's your desk', pointing to its ashes, its remains. Here 'your desk' refers to what is left of a desk and does not imply the continued existence of the desk itself; the person pointing to the ashes would presumably admit (or at least believe) that he had destroyed the desk itself. In a parallel way, then, 'Judd is lying in his coffin' may involve a 'what's left of' use of 'Judd' and may not entail (or at least may not be used with the intention to say) that the person whose remains are being referred to himself still exists.

Earlier I implied that one could coherently hold that one's body is not external to one even though one could survive bodily death. Such a thing is logically or metaphysically possible if one's body is a less important aspect of one than one's psyche and if one's psyche can exist independently of any body. Dualism does not, I think, have to entail the implausible view that a person's body is external to him, even if such a dualist as Descartes did hold such a view. Moreover, I think that ordinary usage, or at least common sense, favours the thesis that a person's body is part of him, or an internal aspect of him, or, at least, not external to him. For example, the fact that we explicitly refer to a dead man's corpse or ashes as his earthly remains indicates that (we believe that) a person's body is not external to him. For the remains of a thing were originally part of, or internal to, that thing. Further evidence for the non-externality thesis comes from some of the ways we commonly compare people. We can say that John and his father resemble each other in their red hair and bad tempers. Normally, it is only with respect to their internal features or aspects that we can say of two things that they resemble (or are like) one another. So the above kind of talk comparing John and his father indicates the belief that a person's body is not external to him.

The naturalness of the above example comparing John and his father tends to show that 'John' has the same reference in 'John is red-haired' as in 'John is bad-tempered', namely, to the being or person John. It tends to show that there is a single being or person John with both physical and mental properties. Our dualism is thus compatible with saying that embodied beings are unities at least in the sense that they have both physical and mental characteristics. And if one wonders how an embodied being can have both a physical and a psychical 'side' and *as a single entity* possess physical characteristics (like red-hairedness) in virtue of (the nature of) its physical side and also psychical characteristics (like bad-temperedness) in virtue of (the nature of) its psychical side, remember that a ship, e.g., can *as a single entity* be both capable of great speed and luxurious, and yet be so in virtue of entirely different parts of itself.

There is reason, then, to think of a person or being's body as part of him, or at least not external to him; and there is also reason to think of embodied beings as 'unities' with both physical and psychical (mental) attributes. But neither of these views seems in any way to impugn the dualism we argued for above.

# 5. States of Affairs

In the present chapter, I shall discuss a kind of entity that I think has been given insufficient attention by philosophers. Entities of the sort I shall be examining I shall call states of affairs (or states, aspects, or features of things). Examples of such states of affairs,[1] aspects of things, etc., are: the redness of Mary's hair, my ability (being able) to speak French, there being ravens, John's proximity to Mary, John's way of walking, and the possibility of her death. We have already, in framing definitions by essence and accident in previous chapters, been making certain explicit or implicit assumptions about the existence conditions and nature of such entities as these (if they exist); and I would like now to discuss the existence conditions and nature of states of affairs, aspects, and the like, in such a way as to justify those assumptions.

A question that immediately arises about such (possible or putative) entities as these is the question how they relate to platonic universals or properties. For example, is the redness of Mary's hair identical with the platonic property or universal Redness, or with the specific platonic universal (shade of Redness), $Redness_n$, that Mary's hair possesses? I think not.[2] For

---

[1] My usage of 'state of affairs', etc., will not always accord with ordinary idiomatic usage. For one thing, in ordinary usage it is more appropriate to talk of states of affairs when a relation between entities is mentioned (proximity between John and Mary) and more appropriate to talk of an aspect when a single entity is mentioned (my ability to speak French).

[2] A number of recent philosophers have argued that (what we are calling)

if there are such entities as platonic universals, they are necessarily existent entities and there is nothing that could or did bring them about or cause them to exist. But the redness of Mary's hair presumably did have a cause, was brought about by certain genes or mutations or what have you, and so it is not identical with any universal like Redness or Redness$_n$. Moreover, such a state of affairs as the redness of Mary's hair is not a necessary existent in the manner of a universal or, for that matter, of a proposition. We cannot say that a certain proposition or universal (or that Redness or Redness$_n$) would never have existed, if certain things had been different. But it is perfectly correct to say that a certain state of affairs (and that the redness of Mary's hair, in particular) would never have existed, if certain things had been different. And that is because such states of affairs as the redness of Mary's hair are contingent entities, if they exist at all. Finally, nothing could put an end to Redness or Redness$_n$, given that these really are necessary existents; but it is perfectly possible that something, e.g., old age or a disease, should put an end to the redness of Mary's hair, so again it would seem that Mary's hair's redness is a contingent non-platonic entity. Thus at least in one sense, the redness of Mary's hair is not a necessarily existent universal (or proposition).

The qualification 'in one sense' is added because there is, I think, another sense in which 'the redness of Mary's hair' means 'that redness that Mary's hair possesses' or 'the specific universal shade of red possessed by Mary's hair'. So in one sense 'the redness of Mary's hair' refers (or purports to refer) to a universal, though in another sense (in which, as we shall see, 'the redness of Mary's hair' is roughly synonymous with 'Mary's hair's being red') 'the redness of Mary's hair' refers (or purports to refer) to what we are calling a state of affairs (or aspect of a thing), and not to a universal. And similarly for such other states of affairs as Helen's beauty, or John's proximity (being near) to Mary: singular referring expressions that are naturally

states of affairs are not universals. See, e.g., D. C. Williams, 'The Elements of Being', *Review of Metaphysics* 7, 1953–54, pp. 1–18, 172–92.

used to refer to or designate them are subject to the above kind of ambiguity, but *we* shall be using them right here solely to refer to states of affairs that are not universals.

Note, incidentally, that in arguing against the identity of certain states of affairs or aspects of things with certain universals (or propositions), I said that since something (logically) can put an end to the redness of Mary's hair, the redness of Mary's hair is a contingently existing entity, and thus not identical with any necessary existent like a universal (or a proposition). A cautious reader might, however, have had doubts about such an argument on the grounds that even if I think only about Redness on Tuesdays, it is (on one natural interpretation) logically possible that something should put an end to the thing I think about on Tuesdays, since I *could* have thought about something destructible on Tuesdays, but that it hardly follows that the thing I (in fact) think about on Tuesdays is a contingent entity, contingently exists. The reason why this does not follow is that 'the thing I think about on Tuesdays' is not (to use a term of Kripke's) a *rigid designator* (of Redness).[3] But what is a rigid designator, and how can that notion be used to bolster my earlier argument that the redness of Mary's hair is a contingent entity, because one can put an end to the redness of Mary's hair?

One can perhaps most simply characterize the notion of rigid designation by saying that a rigid designator is a designator such that if (as it is used in the actual world) it picks out a certain entity in some possible world, then (as it is used in the actual world) it picks out that entity in every possible world in which the entity exists. This condition of rigid designation is, for example, met by canonical designators of universals like 'Redness', since if there is a universal $x$ that 'Redness' (as we use the term) designates in some possible world (e.g., our own), then (as we use the term) 'Redness' designates $x$ in every world

---

[3] Kripke discusses the notion of a rigid designator at length in his 'Identity and Necessity', pp. 144–49.

where $x$ exists. The above condition of rigid designation is not, however, met by 'the thing I think about on Tuesdays', since this designator can pick out an entity $x$ in a possible world where the thing I think about on Tuesdays is $x$ while failing to pick out $x$ in a world where $x$ exists but there is something else $y$ that I think about on Tuesdays.

There is, however, another way of characterizing rigid designation. We can say that if a designator $a$ is rigid, and refers to something actual, then ⌐it is not logically possible that $a$ be something other than the thing that in fact is $a$⌐ will be true. If 'Redness' refers to a real universal, then it meets this condition, because it is not logically possible that Redness be something other than the thing that in fact is Redness. (Or, to put it slightly differently, there is something identical with Redness but no other entity, property, could have been identical with Redness.) On the other hand, 'the thing I think about on Tuesdays' also does not meet this second condition of rigid designation. It is logically possible that the thing I think about on Tuesdays have been something other than the thing I in fact think about on Tuesdays (if there is such a thing).

The reason for mentioning both these conditions of rigid designation is that they are not in general equivalent, even if the differences between them sometimes are not[4] and perhaps need not be worried about. Something can meet the first condition (call it the condition of inclusive rigidity) without meeting the second condition (call it the condition of exclusive rigidity). Consider, for example, the matter of which the sperm I came from was composed; and let us suppose we can give it a name like 'Harry'. Then consider the expression 'the being that came from Harry'. It is an inclusively rigid designator, because (if we assume certain essentialistic views and allow a certain roughness in formulation here) in every possible world where I exist, that

[4] The distinction between these two conditions or kinds of rigidity is, for example, blurred by Kripke in *Identity and Necessity* and in *Naming and Necessity*. But Kripke is aware of their non-equivalence.

expression picks me out. But it is not exclusively rigid, since if the sperm composed of Harry had got together with a different ovum, another being would have been the being that came from Harry. The being that came from Harry might have been someone other than the being that in fact came from Harry.

Nor does exclusive rigidity entail inclusive rigidity. It is not possible that the being that is identical with Nixon and also a politician have been someone other than the being that is in fact identical with Nixon and also a politician, so 'the being that is identical with Nixon and also a politician' is exclusively rigid. But it is not inclusively rigid, since even though it picks out Nixon in the actual world, it does not pick that individual out in worlds where he is apolitical. Of course, we have been assuming here that proper names at least typically[5] function as rigid designators of some kind. In fact, like 'Redness', I think they at least typically function as both inclusively and exclusively rigid. 'Wilfrid Sellars' picks out someone in our world, and (as we use it) it picks out that individual in every world where that individual exists. But it is also not possible that Wilfrid Sellars have been someone other than the being who in fact is Wilfrid Sellars.[6] For similar reasons, I think 'the redness of Mary's hair' (in the sense of 'Mary's hair's being red') is both inclusively and exclusively rigid, whereas 'the state of affairs I think about when I am happy' is neither. Indeed most designators are either both inclusively and exclusively rigid or neither. In general, therefore, I shall call designators rigid when and only when they meet both of these conditions, and shall call them non-

[5] It is by no means clear to me that proper names always have a purely referential use. In *Reason and Scepticism*, p. 49n., for example, I mentioned the example of a woman who was once (and is no longer) Susan Smith, and who is now Susan Jones—all as the result of her marriage to Jones. Kripke ('Naming and Necessity', footnote 25) seems to think such talk is 'loose' and 'sloppy', but I do not see any reason to think so.

[6] Someone else might have been *called* Wilfrid Sellars, and Sellars himself might never have had that name, but that is something different. I assume that it is possible that Sellars exist and not be called Sellars. See 'Naming and Necessity' on these points.

rigid when and only when they meet neither of the conditions. Intermediate cases will not in fact arise in our discussion and I shall not worry about them further.

One cannot go from the *de dicto* interpretation of 'it is possible that something put an end to the thing I think about on Tuesdays' (together with the assumption that the thing I think about on Tuesdays exists) to the *de re* interpretation of the same phrase, which means something like 'there is an $x$ such that I think about $x$ on Tuesdays and something could put an end to $x$' or thus to the conclusion 'the thing I think about on Tuesdays is not a necessary entity'. And the reason why is just that 'the thing I think about on Tuesdays' is not exclusively rigid, that it would have been possible for the thing that I think about on Tuesdays to have been something other than the thing (granting that it exists) that I in fact think about on Tuesdays. However, where $a$ is a rigid designator of an existent entity, ⌜it is logically possible that something put an end to $a$⌝ will be true only if ⌜$a$ is a contingent entity⌝ is also true. If it is possible that something put an end to Cicero, then if Cicero exists at all, there is an $x$ identical with Cicero such that $x$ can have an end put to it, in which case Cicero is a contingently existing entity. Similarly, if it is possible to put an end to the redness of Mary's hair (or it is possible that the redness of Mary's hair not exist), then if in fact the redness of Mary's hair does exist, the redness of Mary's hair is a state of affairs to which an end can be put, something that need not exist, that is contingently existent. With rigid designators, we can go from modality *de dicto* to modality *de re* (with appropriate existence assumptions); and I think it could be easily enough shown that when one uses such designators, one can also argue from modality *de re* to modality *de dicto* (with appropriate existence qualifications). And given these conclusions, it should, I think, be pretty clear that our earlier argument from the fact that it is possible to put an end to the redness of Mary's hair to the conclusion that such a state of affairs is not identical with any (necessarily existent) platonic universal or proposition, is a perfectly reasonable one.

Note, finally, that our arguments against the identity of certain states of affairs with universals or propositions depended on pointing out that various states of affairs, unlike universals or propositions as traditionally conceived, exist only contingently and can be causally affected by events in the world. And this tends to show that states of affairs are less suspicious, less perplexing, and less 'queer' as putative entities than are universals or propositions. One reason why the existence of universals and propositions has been so suspect among so many philosophers has been their supposed necessary existence and causal isolation. And so to the extent that we have shown that various states of affairs lack these properties, if they exist at all, there is at least not this kind of reason for supposing that such entities do not exist, and that is some justification for not making the validity of our definitions by essence and accident depend on the impossibility of there being states of affairs and for examining the nature and existence conditions of various kinds of states of affairs in order to see how to exclude them from falling under certain of our definitions in this book.

## II

In this section, I would like to discuss some of the various different kinds of states of affairs (or aspects of things) that may exist in the universe. So far the emphasis has been on one particular kind of state of affairs, states of the sort represented by the redness of Mary's hair. Other states of affairs of this kind include: my ability to speak French, John's proximity to Mary, and Helen's beauty. All such states of affairs have something in common. As we normally use phrases like 'the redness of Mary's hair', the redness of Mary's hair exists (if such a thing can exist at all) when and only when Mary's hair is red; similarly, my ability to speak French exists (if it can exist at all) just when I am able (in some appropriate sense) to speak French, and Helen's beauty exists and lasts, if at all, precisely as long as Helen is beautiful. Such claims seem tautologous, and that, I think, is because they express what is analytic of such phrases as 'the redness of Mary's hair', 'my ability to speak French', etc., at least on *one* natural reading of such phrases.

In effect, the kind of states of affairs (or aspects of things) that we have been dealing with thus far are all of them (rigidly) designated by phrases of the form 'the $f$ness (or $f$ity) of $x$' or of the form '$x$'s $f$ness (or $f$ity)', where it is thought to be *necessary that* the $f$ness of $x$ (or $x$'s $f$ness, etc.) exist when and only when $x$ is $f$ and where it is thought that if the $f$ness of $x$ exists at all, the $f$ness of $x$ *essentially*: exists when and only when $x$ is $f$. (All this could be put more accurately, but less simply, in terms of corners.) Phrases of the form '$x$'s $f$ness', etc., are, in fact, subject to rather confusing, but nonetheless interesting ambiguities, however. As we shall see shortly, and have in part seen already, although in many cases talk about the $f$ness of $x$ obeys the 'logic' just described, in other cases it does not, and that is because in such cases, phrases of the form 'the $f$ness of $x$' or '$x$'s $f$ness', etc., designate different sorts of states of affairs from those they designate in the cases whose logic we have just briefly been discussing.

However, there do seem to be clear cases where phrases like '$x$'s $f$ness' designate (or purport to designate) states of affairs that exist when and only when $x$ is $f$. Now this means that in such cases, if something $x$ is $f$, then not $f$, and still later $f$ again, one and the same thing, the $f$ness of $x$, exists, temporarily ceases to exist, and then exists again later. And it might be objected at this point that it is impossible in principle for one and the same thing to exist, cease to exist, and then later exist once again. But this last thesis is normally put forward only with regard to concrete entities like tables, buildings, flowers, or people, and might well precisely *not* apply to such other sorts of things as states of affairs or aspects. Nor is the thesis very convincing even with regard to concrete entities. If a certain building were destroyed and the stones of which it was made scattered all over so that no one knew their whereabouts, then the building would no longer exist. But is it not conceivable that a later archaeologist should accidentally find some of the stones, track down the others, and reconstruct the building pretty much as it originally was from the stones that were originally in it? And is this not a plausible case where a building that once existed and then ceased to exist exists once again? The thesis has very little force if any, then, against what I have been saying about states of affairs and their coming back into existence. Moreover, usage strongly suggests that states of affairs exist, cease to exist, and then exist again. We imply this kind of thing, for example, when we speak of a certain vampire's need (or yearning) for blood existing whenever the moon is full, but not at other times, or when we say that a certain pill will put an end *temporarily* to someone's desire (craving) for sugar.[7]

I think, then, that there is every reason to hold that there are many cases in which phrases of the form '$x$'s $f$ness' or 'the $f$ness of $x$' (purport to) refer to states of affairs (or aspects) that exist precisely when $x$ is $f$. In those cases, furthermore, I think '$x$'s $f$ness' or 'the $f$ness of $x$' is used to mean something like '$x$'s being $f$' or 'the being $f$ of $x$'.[8] 'Helen's beauty' can be used to mean pretty much the same as 'Helen's being beautiful' and 'the redness of Mary's hair' to mean much the same as 'Mary's hair's being red'. One reason to believe this is the fairly obvious equivalence in meaning of '(the property of) beauty' and '(the property of) being beautiful'. Further evidence is the seemingly tautological character of the claim that (of necessity) something

---

[7] Because states of affairs can cease to exist temporarily, there can be *instances* of a single state of affairs. Thus there can be various (unrepeatable) instances of John's drunkenness (being drunk), existing on different occasions. And John's drunken *stupors* are precisely just these *instances* of John's being drunk.

[8] I assume that phrases of the form '$x$'s $f$ing' are to be understood in a way parallel to the way in which we understand phrases of the form '$x$'s being $f$'. Thus the state of affairs my living in Paris exists, if such a thing can exist at all, just when I am living in Paris. Similarly, the event, process, state of affairs, or what-have-you $a$'s changing from green to brown exists just when $a$ is changing from green to brown.

brings about (or puts an end to) Helen's beauty if and only if it brings about (or puts an end to) Helen's being beautiful. Or consider the similarly tautologous character of: (of necessity) something results from the redness of Mary's hair just in case it results from Mary's hair's being red.

The only difficulty with identifying, e.g., Helen's beauty and Helen's being beautiful, in the appropriate senses, seems to me to be the fact that it is perfectly acceptable to say that Helen's beauty will not last forever, but odd to say that Helen's being beautiful will not last forever. But what sounds odd may still, as far as anyone has ever shown, be meaningful and true. And perhaps this is the case with 'Helen's being beautiful will not last forever' and certain similar locutions. Indeed I think we have reason to think that something like this is the case in the present instance, given the meaningfulness and putative truth of 'something will sooner or later put an end to Helen's being beautiful' and the plausible general view that one can only put an end to something if it exists but does not last (exist) forever. And if that is so, we can perhaps plausibly hold that Helen's beauty and Helen's being beautiful are the same state of affairs.

On the other hand, the oddness of the phrase mentioned above may make one decide that there cannot *be* such an *entity* as Helen's being beautiful, and that 'Helen's being beautiful' only appears to be a referring expression because of its misleading use in such phrases as 'this will put an end to Helen's being beautiful'. But whatever one decides, it should at least be reasonable to conclude that 'Helen's being beautiful' does not refer to something other than Helen's beauty. If that expression is referential, then by virtue of its very meaning it (rigidly) designates what 'Helen's beauty' (rigidly) designates. In any case, I shall not make anything important depend on assuming such referentiality.

Phrases like 'Helen's beauty' and 'the redness of Mary's hair' are ambiguous not only because they can be used to refer either to specific universals or to states of affairs of the kind we have been discussing, but also because they can be used to refer to *facts*. 'His wife's infidelity', for example, surely refers to a fact in 'he was informed of his wife's infidelity', where we seem to be saying something with the same meaning as 'he was informed of the fact that his wife was unfaithful'. However, if I say that someone's wife's infidelity will continue until he is cured of his impotence, we cannot substitute 'the fact that his wife is being unfaithful' for 'his wife's infidelity' and get natural-sounding English. This is some evidence that 'his wife's infidelity' and other such phrases can refer both to facts and to states of affairs that are not facts.[9] More precise clarification of the difference between states of affairs like those we have been examining and facts will have to await our next chapter, which is chiefly devoted to the nature and existence conditions of facts.

There are certain interesting sorts of states of affairs that we have still not mentioned. Consider, for example, the difference between Helen's beauty and Helen's *present* beauty. If Helen will always be beautiful, but will later on not be *as* beautiful as she now is, Helen's beauty will last longer than Helen's present beauty. If Helen is beautiful in a certain way and to a certain degree at present, then Helen's present beauty essentially: exists just if (and when) she is beautiful in that way and to that degree. Helen's beauty neither depends on, nor is identical with, Helen's present beauty, even if the latter does depend on the former. The states of affairs referred to by such phrases as 'Helen's present beauty' can be referred to in other ways as well. Thus, for example, 'Helen's present way of being beautiful'—if it is a referring expression at all—can be used to refer to what 'Helen's present beauty' refers to. The two phrases seem to refer to mutually logically dependent states of affairs—by virtue of their very meaning. In addition, 'Helen's present looks' (or, perhaps, 'Helen's present appearance') seems capable of designating Helen's present beauty.

Helen's present beauty (or looks) can, moreover, be referred

[9] Cf. Moore, *Philosophical Papers*, London: Allen and Unwin, 1959, pp. 80ff.

to by such phrases as: 'the (present) state of Helen's beauty (or looks)'. For in general phrases of the form 'the present state of $x$' are codesignative with phrases of the form 'the way $x$ is (on the whole) at present'. Thus the present state of the universe (or of my body) is just the way the universe (or my body) is (on the whole) at present. Finally, it should be pointed out that phrases of the form '$x$'s present way of $f$ing' may designate what phrases of the form '$x$'s $f$ing the way it does at present' designate. The police's present way of handling riots may perhaps be the same as the police's handling riots the way they do at present (and, in addition, *is* the same as the police's present riot handling).

We have seen that phrases using gerund forms or obvious nominalizations of such phrases using special endings like 'ness', 'ty', 'hood' and 'ance' can be used in referring to states of affairs. But such reference can also be made by other sorts of phrases. 'Helen's present looks', for example, refers to the way that Helen looks at present and involves a nominalization of the verb 'to look'; but it makes use of no special nominalization ending like 'ness', 'ty', etc. There are numerous such cases. For example, my needing love can be referred to by 'my need for love' and my living in Paris by 'my life in Paris'.

Phrases like 'Helen's present beauty' refer non-rigidly. And the states of affairs they designate are all incapable of alteration. Helen's present beauty cannot alter without lasting. But of necessity, if Helen's present beauty alters, Helen ceases to be beautiful in the way she now is and her present beauty does not last. So there are inconsistent necessary conditions of Helen's present beauty's altering. Since it is necessary that any such specific state of an entity not alter and Helen's present beauty is essentially specific, Helen's present beauty is (logically) immutable, is an essentially unaltering state or feature of Helen.

On the other hand, I am inclined to think that Helen's beauty *can* alter, even if Helen's present beauty cannot. The evidence for this is not merely the fact that we speak of Helen's beauty altering over the years in a way that we would *not* speak of Helen's present beauty altering over the years. For after all, we do speak of the contents of a certain box altering (over time) having in mind the thought not that certain things in the box have themselves undergone alteration, but rather that certain things in the box have been exchanged for or replaced by others. And it would be possible to hold that in speaking of alteration in Helen's beauty all that is really meant is that one way in which Helen is beautiful (one state of Helen's beauty) is exchanged for or replaced by another, rather than that her beauty itself undergoes alteration (in what it is like). But I think this would be a mistake, because the analogy with alteration in the contents of a box is not a very good one. For one thing, we can say that Helen's beauty has become more autumnal and less vivid over the years, or that her beauty is less brilliant than *it* was. But when the festive clothes in a box are replaced by drabber ones, it would be unnatural or misleading to describe what has happened by saying that the contents of the box have become drabber, or that the contents are drabber than *they* were. The best explanation of this latter fact seems just to consist in the fact that when the contents of a box are just replaced, they need not have undergone alteration themselves. And the fact that we do allow ourselves to speak of Helen's beauty becoming more autumnal over the years or of Helen's beauty being less vivid or brilliant than it formerly was seems definitely to favor the assumption that a state of affairs like Helen's beauty (Helen's being beautiful) is not immutable.

There remains at least one important kind of state of affairs that we have not discussed in the present chapter. These are states of affairs that are designated by phrases resulting from the nominalization of various existence claims, states of affairs like there being ravens, or the existence (existing) of ravens. If such phrases as 'the existence of ravens' or 'there being ravens' are referring phrases at all, then I think that they have the same reference and that they refer to the species or kind raven. To put an end to the existence of ravens, or to there being ravens, is *ipso facto* to put an end to the species or kind raven, to raven-kind. (I use 'there are ravens' to mean 'there is at least one raven', so there is such a thing as there being ravens, presumably, if there is at least one raven.) The existence conditions of there being ravens or of the existence of ravens seem the same as those of the species raven itself, and as far as I can see there is no reason not to say that there is only one entity here that can be designated in different ways.

Presumably, the species raven can alter, just as the human species has altered over the millenia. The human species is a less hairy species of animal than it was fifty thousand years ago, physical anthropologists claim. In that case, the existence of ravens and there being ravens are mutable states of affairs, given their identity with the species raven.[10]

[10] In the light of these facts about the possiblity of alteration in states of affairs and in species in particular, we are now, perhaps, in a position to rule out certain counterexamples to our earlier definition of the physical that we have delayed considering till now. Consider the class of events (the species event), and compare it with the class of physical events (the species physical event). Surely the former is not physical and the latter is, but both meet our earlier conditions (a), (b) and (c) of physicalness. The difference between these two entities is hard to spell out, but perhaps it can be done as follows: Consider the species physical event, and consider the putative entity: the way the species physical event is at $t$ (where '$t$' refers to a particular time). As we saw earlier, the latter entity has to be thought of as immutable and as depending on the species physical event. As long as the species physical event exists, such other entities will also presumably exist; if there is a species then there will be such a thing as its way of being at some given time (its state at that time). But such a state clearly may at most accidentally exist in a universe where there are selves: the class of physical events can remain as it is at a given time long after that time, no matter what beings exist or do not exist after that time.

However, consider the class of events. If there are psychic events at $t$ and not at $t'$, then that class has altered between those times, just as the human species alters if most men are hairy at one time and not at another. But consider the state of the class of events at a time when there are mental events. That state can only last if psychic or mental events, and hence selves, continue to exist. And indeed it is possible that at a given time $t_0$ every immutable entity dependent on the species event essentially exists

It should be clear that I am treating various species, classes, races, kinds, etc., as non-abstract entities (or, at least, as atypical abstract entities) that can alter, can perish, etc. Some philosophers, e.g., Quine, identify species and kinds with logicians' classes or sets and thus consider them abstract entities;[11] but this is unfair to the way we ordinarily conceive species and to the way biologists typically consider them. Biologists and ordinary

only when selves do. Thus, for example, if there are at $t_0$ psychic events and a table $a$, then there is such a thing as the way the class of events and table $a$ are at $t_0$; but this entity too will essentially exist only when selves do. Finally, consider the entity: either-the-class-of-events-or-table-$a$-existing, which could alternatively be described as: the class of things identical either with the class of events or with table $a$. Now classes or species, when understood on the biological model, alter when their members alter or cease to exist in certain ways, etc. The class of mammals alters as (enough) individual mammals alter. So the class of things identical with either the class of events or with table $a$ could alter if the class of events altered. In that case, if there are psychic events at $t_0$, the way the class of things identical with either the class of events or table $a$ is at $t_0$ will constitute a putative entity that essentially: exists only when there are psychic events and selves at the same time.

What all this tends to show, I think, is that the following condition (d) is analytic of physicality and distinguishes the class of physical events from such non-physical entities as the class of events. $X$ is physical only if (d) it is not possible that everything $y$ that is immutable and dependent on $x$ be essentially: existent only when selves or beings exist. Our earlier conditions (a), (b), and (c), taken together with this new condition (d), are, I think, necessary and sufficient for the definition of physicalness. I am inclined, then, to offer as our final definition of physicalness:

* ⌜$a$ is physical⌝ means about the same as ⌜there is an $x$ identical with $a$ such that $x$ is at most accidentally existent only if some self exists at some time; $x$ is essentially not depended on by any self, and is not essentially: existent if there ever is an experience; $x$ is not essentially: existent at every time when something exists but no beings exist; $x$ is located in space, and can be located in some places but not in others, but is not identical with Space or Time, any part or interval of Space or Time, any point or moment of Space or Time, etc.; and it is not possible that everything $y$ that is immutable and dependent on $x$ be essentially: existent only when selves or beings exist⌝.

[11] Cf. his *Methods of Logic*, N.Y.: Holt, 1959, p. 204f.

people talk about the origin of species and about the destruction of species. And they also speak of species as if they occupied regions of space, e.g., certain parts of Africa, and could migrate, etc. All this also holds true of families, classes, etc., in the biological (type of) usage of these terms. In particular, biologists' classes are not the classes logicians talk about: they are very differently conceived. For the biologist there is no such thing as the class (or species) unicorn, but for the typical logician who countenances classes, the class of unicorns is the null class and exists if other classes do. Furthermore, any logicians' classes with the same members are thought of as identical. But this is not so in biological usage. Biologists distinguish the floral species *Amaryllis formosissima* from the genus *Amaryllis*, even though (I am informed) it is the only species of that genus and no one, presumably, assumes that someday there (probably) will be other species of that genus. I think that biologists probably implicitly assume that mutual logical dependence is necessary to identity and do not consider any species (like *Amaryllis formosissima*) identical with any genus (like *Amaryllis*) that does not logically depend on it; and the latter does not depend on the former because it (logically) *could* include other species and exist 'through' them while the former perished. The same holds true, I think, for classes and orders, where a given order is always the only order of some class; the order and class would still not be identical because of the possibility of there having instead been other orders included in that class.[12] I am not saying that logicians do not require mutual logical dependence for class identity, but rather only that sameness of actual membership is not sufficient for mutual dependence or identity of biological-type classes (and species), so that if sameness of actual membership is sufficient for the identity of logicians' classes (and thus,

[12] Biological species and classes are like social organizations, in as much as it is clearly possible for two such organizations to have the same members. Cf. Sellars, 'Grammar and Existence: a Preface to Ontology', in *Science, Perception, and Reality*, London: Routledge and Kegan Paul, 1963, p. 254.

on our assumption, for their mutual dependence), such classes must be very different in their nature from biological-type classes (and species). Moreover, we have discovered ample reason to think that biological-type classes and the like are not typical abstract entities in any traditional sense of the term.

## III

I briefly argued, above, that the species raven, there being ravens, and the existence of ravens were all one and the same thing—if they existed. Such a claim may seem odd or hard to understand, and I would like to say some more about it, and about the reasoning behind some of our other identity claims, in what follows.

I said that the species raven and there being ravens, e.g., have the same existence conditions, and that this gives us some reason to think them identical, if they exist at all. This should be spelled out more clearly. There being ravens and the species raven are mutually logically dependent, if they exist. Neither one of them *can* exist at a time when the other does not, if they both *do* exist. Now earlier we argued that mutual logical dependence is necessary to identity. But I also want to hold that with respect to a large class of entities, including the species raven and there being ravens, mutual logical dependence is *sufficient* for identity as well. This is my chief reason for claiming that the species raven and there being ravens are identical.

That mutual logical dependence is not in every case sufficient for identity is clear from the fact that this would make all necessary existences, all propositions and universals, etc., count as a single entity.[13] I am also very unclear about whether mutual logical dependence is sufficient for identity even among con-

---

[13] I tend to hold that necessary entities are not outside time, but rather have to exist *at* all times. All the arguments against this view seem to me to be weak. However, everything we are saying here could, where necessary, be adjusted to the assumption that necessary entities are not in time.

tingent entities. One of my worries concerns the ontological category of facts. In the next chapter we shall see that facts are, many of them, contingent entities, but that even contingently existing facts are extremely similar to necessary entities in the *rigidity* of the conditions of their persistence or continued existence. And this, I think, has a great deal to do with what makes one in many cases reluctant to call certain mutually dependent contingent facts identical. (I shall say more about problems with facts later on.) The conditions of the persistence of space-time worms seem to be just as rigid as those of facts, and mutual logical dependence does not appear to be sufficient for their identity either. Because of their rigid persistence conditions both facts and worms (as well as all necessary existents) are what I shall later call temporally bound entities. And I wish to claim only that mutual logical dependence is sufficient for the identity of (temporally unbound) contingent entities other than facts or worms.

The necessity of mutual dependence for the identity of entities in general clearly follows from Leibniz's Law and the acceptance of *de re* modality, of quantification into modal contexts. It seems much less controversial than the assumption that mutual dependence is sufficient for the identity of contingent entities other than facts or worms.[14] Of course, there are reasons of ontological simplifying deriving from Ockham's Razor for assuming such sufficiency. Indeed, as far as I can tell, Ockham was the first philosopher to suggest that (something like)

[14] But the view that mutual logical dependence is needed for identity may cause many philosophers to revise their assumptions about which states of affairs are identical to which. E.g., even if Nader is my favorite American, Nader's being happy is not the same as my favorite American's being happy, at least on one very natural reading of those phrases, since the two states of affairs are not (on that reading) mutually dependent. Indeed, our whole approach suggests that in deciding whether ⌜$a$'s being $f$⌝ and ⌜$b$'s being $g$⌝ are codesignative, considering whether $a$ and $b$ or ⌜being $f$⌝ and ⌜being $g$⌝ have the same reference is less important than considering the *de re* modal relations that obtain between the states of affairs that are in fact designated by ⌜$a$'s being $f$⌝ and ⌜$b$'s being $g$⌝.

mutual dependence was sufficient for identity.[15] But as soon as one assumes the sufficiency of mutual dependence for the identity of contingent entities other than facts or worms, one runs into controversial or implausible consequences.

One such consequence is that Catiline's being near Tully is identical with, the same state of affairs as, Catiline's being near Cicero.[16] For it might seem that even if these are mutually dependent, they cannot be identical. After all, the *fact* or *proposition* that Catiline is near Tully seems definitely not to be the same as the *fact* or *proposition* that Catiline is near Cicero (even though these facts or propositions are mutually dependent). It is not clear to me what the right answer is about this question of fact or proposition identity, but in any case we are here not dealing with facts or propositions, but with states of affairs which, we have seen and shall be seeing, are very different in their manner of existence from facts or propositions. So perhaps certain states of affairs can be identical, even if facts or propositions 'corresponding' to them are not.

Of course, if what I am saying is correct, then 'Catiline's being near Tully' and 'Catiline's being near Cicero' are non-synonymous rigid designators of identical states of affairs. And one might doubt whether such a thing is possible. But consider a case in which Peter and Harry are one and the same tenth century man and Peter (Harry) is the only canonized saint of that century. Knowing these facts, one might say: 'the tenth century was particularly bleak, from a religious standpoint, in the West; indeed, there was only one saintly life (led) in that century.' Since it is natural to say this, it must be natural to think Harry's life and Peter's life are one and the same (life); and 'Peter's life' and 'Harry's life' are presumably rigid designators of states of affairs that are not synonymous. But then is there anything to prevent us from saying that 'Catiline's being near

---

[15] In *Summa Totius Logicae* III, II, c. xxvii, in *Ockham: Philosophical Writings*, Indianapolis: Bobbs-Merrill, 1964, p. 103f.

[16] I assume that it is necessary that if Cicero exists, Cicero is identical with Tully. Cf. *Reason and Scepticism*, Ch. 1, sect. 2; and Kripke, *op.cit.*

Cicero' and 'Catiline's being near Tully' are non-synonymous rigid designators of one and the same state of affairs?

Our assumption of the sufficiency of mutual dependence for the identity of contingent entities other than worms or facts also yields the controversial conclusion that one is one's own existence, that I, for example, am my existence, my existing. The view that one is one's existence was, quite understandably, espoused by Ockham;[17] it was also held by Jean Buridan.[18]

One objection to identifying me with my existence, and thus to the sufficiency of mutual dependence for the identity of contingent non-facts, is that 'my existence' refers to an aspect or feature of me, or a state of affairs involving (depending on) me; and I am no (mere) aspect or feature of things or of myself, nor a state of affairs (involving myself). I am a person, a being, not not an aspect of or state of affairs involving such an entity. But I am not assuming that my usage of 'state of affairs' or 'aspect' strictly conforms to ordinary usage; it may in some sense, rather, 'round out' such ordinary usage of those expressions. And perhaps there is nothing so very odd in saying that a person is identical with what is an aspect or state of affairs in a 'rounded out' or 'stretched' sense of 'aspect' or 'state of affairs', or in saying that a person is identical with what is an aspect or state of affairs of an odd sort.[19]

More worrisome, perhaps, is the thought that if I am my existence, then if I give a lecture, my existence gives a lecture. For it is certainly easy to balk at the thought that one's existence

---

[17] *Op. cit.*

[18] In 'Questions on Aristotle's Metaphysics' in Walsh and Hyman, eds., *Philosophy in the Middle Ages*, N.Y.: Harper and Row, 1967, pp. 713ff. The view has also been denied by many philosophers, e.g., Brentano in 'Genuine and Fictitious Objects' in Chisholm, ed., *Realism and the Background of Phenomenology*, Glencoe: Free Press, 1960, pp. 71–5.

[19] This type of answer will perhaps also serve to reply to those who complain that on my view of the conditions of identity, I am identical with my unit-species. But a unit species is presumably only a species in a 'stretched' or 'rounded' sense, or a very odd or deviant sort of species, and it is perhaps not so strange that I should be identical with *such* a species.

gives (or even could give) a lecture. Of course, it is odd to talk of one's existence giving a lecture. But as we said earlier, oddness can be compatible with truth and meaningfulness.[20] Perhaps it is odd, but nonetheless meaningful and accurate, to say that one's existence gives (can give) a lecture. And one will have reason to (want to) say just this sort of thing, if one has reason to (want to) treat mutual dependence as sufficient for identity over a broad area. And we do have reason to (want to) treat mutual dependence as broadly sufficient for identity. Doing so allows one ontological simplification (or reduction) of a sort generally presumed to be desirable, e.g., in Ockham's Razor. One has fewer different entities to worry about. Moreover, the view that mutual logical dependence is sufficient for identity with respect to contingent entities other than facts or worms has an appealing neatness and clarity about it, especially considering that a single easily statable condition—mutual logical dependence—becomes both necessary and sufficient for identity over a broad spectrum of entities that includes most of the entities that most philosophers are most interested in. And the view has a certain *initial* intuitive plausibility (aside from any implausibility the conclusions it leads us to may have) that explains why philosophers like Ockham (and later Hume) were inclined to accept it. I think, then, that we have certain general philosophical reasons for believing in the sufficiency of mutual logical dependence for the identity of contingent, temporally unbound entities, and thus for believing that one's existence can give a lecture, and is identical with oneself, despite the initial oddness of saying so.[21] And, in addition, I think there is at least one, more direct, kind of reason for saying that one is one's existence. In rather old-fashioned or literary English, we

[20] Cf. J. Fodor, *Psychological Explanation*, N.Y.: Random House, 1968, pp. 100–6. Fodor discusses many cases where oddness seems compatible with meaningfulness and truth.

[21] It is odd, but meaningful and true, to say that a certain *entity* is giving a lecture. The view I am tentatively arguing for attributes to 'my existence is giving a lecture' the same kind of *innocuous* oddness.

often speak of tables, persons, etc., as 'existences'. But if I am *an* existence, in that sense, then that is surely some support for saying that I am *my* (own) existence. All in all, I think we have definite reason to accept the idea that mutual logical dependence is sufficient (and not just necessary) for the identity of contingent entities other than worms or facts, or at least to assume (or feign the assumption of) such sufficiency, in order to see where it leads us in putting together a metaphysical view of things.[22]

[22] One problem with the sufficiency of mutual dependence that we have not mentioned and that we can only discuss briefly is that it leads to holding that 'my existing (existence) in a world where two and two are four' refers to the same state of affairs as 'my existing (existence) in a world where I am not a prime number'. Note that we are here referring to states of affairs other than facts. Perhaps one should instead talk of me-existing-in-a-world-where-two-and-two-are-four and of me-existing-in-a-world-where-I-am-not-a-prime-number. And is it really plausible to think that we here have *two different* on-going states of affairs in the world? (I assume that $x$'s being $f$ can be the same as $x$'s being $g$, even if $f$ness is not $g$ness. After all, Cicero's being near Cicero and Catiline seems to be the same as Cicero's being near Catiline. Indeed, *Cicero's* being near Catiline seems to be the same as *Catiline's* being near Cicero.)

# 6. Facts

I

Facts, I have already suggested, are very different from the states of affairs we discussed in Chapter 5. And I would like now to be more specific and systematic about these differences, and about the nature of facts in general, than I have previously been.

Our chief problem is to describe the nature and existence conditions of those entities, if any, that are referred to by phrases of the form 'the fact that *p*'. Such phrases purport to refer, and I shall treat them as if they did. It is often held that facts have spatial location in the world. Both Wittgenstein in the *Tractatus*[1] and Russell in *Logic and Knowledge*[2] seem to have held that facts were spatially located and that physical entities like tables and chairs were constituents of facts like the fact that the table is near the chair. The oddness of conceiving facts this way has been pointed out by Zeno Vendler, among others, in recent years.[3] It is odd to say that the fact that the table exists is (near) where the table is; but, on the other hand, it cannot be far from the table either. Nor does it seem to make much sense to say that the fact that the table is brown is near the fact that the table is heavy. The oddness or strangeness of these ways of speaking is evidence, but not proof, that facts lack particular spatial location. But any theory of facts should, I think,

[1] Cf. G. Pitcher, *The Philosophy of Wittgenstein*, Englewood Cliffs: Prentice-Hall, 1964, p. 20.

[2] London: Allen and Unwin, 1956, pp. 187, 214, 270.

[3] 'Facts and Events' in *Linguistics in Philosophy*, Cornell U. Press, 1967, p. 142.

endeavor to explain this oddness; and the theory to be presented here will not only explain the oddness, but also explain why facts indeed do lack specific location (in one place rather than another).

In any case, the spatial location of facts seems more problematic than that of states of affairs of the sort discussed in the last chapter. After all we seem to locate Helen's beauty in particular places when we say that it is only skin deep. And saying that Kant's life was led entirely within 200 miles of Koenigsberg, or that a certain diplomat carries his bad temper around with him wherever he goes, seems to be ascribing spatial location to such states of affairs as lives and tempers. (Presumably, a man's bad temper is identical with his being bad-tempered.) So one thing our theory of facts should help us to explain is why it seems so much more natural to ascribe particular location to states of affairs of the kind we have already discussed than to facts.

Facts, then, are somewhat 'queer' entities; there is something a little bit queer about entities that seem to lack spatial location. Another 'queer' aspect of facts is that one cannot destroy a fact. Consider the fact that there are (tenselessly) men. If, indeed, such a fact exists, what could possibly put an end to its existence? One could destroy the human race, mankind, humanity, put an end to the existence of men; but one cannot cause the end of the fact that there are men *at some time or other*. It is, perhaps, conceivable that one should bring it about that no such fact ever exists; but once, or if, such a fact (ever) exists, its destruction is impossible.[4] At least this is how we tend to talk and think about facts. Perhaps we can get a clearer insight into why facts cannot be destroyed, if we remember the intimate connection that has always been thought to exist between facts and propositions. For whatever other differences there have been among philosophers as to the nature of facts, they have almost always agreed that of necessity there is a fact that *p* just as long as the proposition that *p* is true. And a

---

[4] Cf. Vendler, *op. cit.*, pp. 142–6.

proposition like the proposition that there are men at some time is clearly such that if it is ever true, it is always true thereafter. Such a proposition cannot be true, and then become false (or untrue) or cease to be; and so the fact corresponding to that proposition cannot, it would seem, be destroyed or in any other way cease to be.

So far we have only mentioned the sort of tenseless facts that correspond to tenseless propositions. What, for example, about the fact that the Russian navy now exists, and the tensed proposition to which it corresponds? Can one cause *such* facts to go out of existence?[5] I think not; it would seem that it is always too late to put an end to the fact that the Russian navy now exists. For one can put an end only to what already exists, and if that fact exists, then the proposition that the Russian navy now exists is true, in which case the most we can do is to prevent it from being the case that the Russian navy exist later, after now, i.e., prevent its existence at some *later* now.

But even if we cannot *put an end* to tensed or tenseless facts, it may be possible that tensed facts should *cease to exist*, in the light of the following considerations. A fact, of necessity, exists only as long as the proposition that corresponds to it exists. But some philosophers have held that the proposition that the Russian navy now exists can only be asserted right now, and one might hold that a proposition cannot continue to exist when it is no longer (even) assertible in principle. From these thoughts the conclusion would follow that the fact that the Russian navy now exists (and the proposition that the Russian navy now exists) exists only at the present moment and so can and does cease to exist. Of course, such ceasing to be would occur by

[5] By 'the proposition or fact that the Russian navy now exists', I mean to refer to a particular time. E.g., the proposition that the Russian navy now exists is true now and will not become false because the Russian navy fails to exist at some later time (some later now). This accords with current philosophical usage; but there is an ordinary and sometime philosophical usage of 'the proposition that the Russian navy now exists' in which that phrase refers to something that can be true and then later false. I shall avoid this latter usage.

virtue of the very passage of time, and this ceasing to be cannot be brought about by *us*, by anything we *do*. So even given the present train of reasoning, it remains true that we cannot (by actions) put an end to any facts.

The above argument is, however, open to doubt on various counts. Why should propositions have to cease to be when not assertible? And is it really so obvious that one can never later express the very proposition that one now asserts when one says 'the Russian navy now exists'? Many philosophers have held, on the contrary, that that proposition can later be asserted by using the past-tense 'the Russian navy existed then' or the tenseless 'the Russian navy exists at that time';[6] and I tend myself to be very sympathetic to this point of view. In any case, it is hardly *clear* that tensed propositions have to or even can cease to exist, given the present difficulty of answering certain crucial questions about the identity-conditions and the general nature of propositions. But at least the following can be said about both tensed and untensed facts: all facts either essentially do not go out of existence or are such that for some time *t* they essentially exist only at *t* (and essentially do not last after *t*). For tenseless propositions cannot cease to be; and tensed propositions either cannot go out of existence or have to go out of existence with the passage of time (and have to exist only at a certain particular time if they exist at all), because despite our philosophical ignorance in these matters, it seems to be an entirely non-contingent question whether propositions can exist only if assertible and whether the proposition now asserted by 'the Russian navy now exists' can be asserted later.

Given these facts about facts, we can see how ontologically different facts are from states of affairs of the kind described in Chapter 5. Helen's beauty can be destroyed (by something other than the passage of time) and does not essentially exist forever once it exists. Helen's beauty can exist at more than one time, and it is entirely contingent when and whether Helen's

[6] E.g., Frege in 'The Thought; a Logical Inquiry' in Strawson, ed., *Philosophical Logic*, London: Oxford, 1967, p. 24.

beauty ceases to be. And the same can be said for tables, beings, bad tempers, lives, etc., as far as their *going out of existence* is concerned. Facts, however, are such that it is entirely non-contingent when and whether they cease to be, with the passage of time. And we have just seen in some detail why this is so.

Many philosophers have been confused or misguided about the difference between facts and states of affairs of the sort discussed in the last chapter. For example, some philosophers have held views about facts in accordance with which my being white (or my whiteness) and the fact that I am white (now) are one and the same entity.[7] But since we can put an end to the former but not to the latter, the entities are not possessed of the same modal properties and are not identical. Furthermore, my being white essentially lasts while, but only while, I am white, whereas the fact that I am white now either essentially does not cease to be or else essentially exists only right now. So such entities as my being white and the fact that I am now white are not, if they exist, mutually logically dependent, and, if so, definitely not identical.

It is also a common misconception that my being white is identical with my being white now. But the latter cannot have an end put to it (except, perhaps, by time's passage), whereas the former can be destroyed by many things other than time, so they do not have the same modal-causal properties. Moreover, my whiteness or my being white is a state of affairs (or aspect of me) that can exist for a while, cease to exist, and then exist again; but it seems to make no sense at all to conceive such a thing occurring to my being white now. The very simple reason, I think, why my being white (my whiteness) is not my being white now is that the latter just *is* the fact that I am white (now). Everything we have said about the fact that I am white (now) also seems to apply to my being white now (if there is such an entity). The fact that I am white (now) cannot *temporarily* cease to be; and neither, it seems, can my being white now; the

[7] E.g., C. Baylis in 'Facts, Propositions, Exemplification, and Truth', *Mind* 57, 1948, p. 461f.

existence conditions of the two putative entities seem equally rigid or restrictive. Moreover, 'the fact that I am white now' and 'my being white now' seem very similar in meaning and seem to fit equally well in a large variety of contexts or expressions ('he is unaware of the fact that I am white now' and 'he is unaware of my being white now'). And this similarity or sameness of meaning also seems responsible for the mutual dependence of my being white now and the fact that I am white. So I shall tentatively assume, in what follows, that these entities are identical, if existent at all.

It would seem, then, that my being white is not my being white now.[8] And for similar reasons, my being white is also not my being white at some time or other. In addition, my being white now (at present) is not the same thing as my present whiteness. Some physiological process can and will put an end to my present whiteness, to my present way of being white; but no such process could put an end to my being white at present, to the fact that I am now white. This fact either essentially exists only at one time or else essentially does not cease to be, whereas my present whiteness has neither of these modal properties. They are neither mutually dependent nor identical.

## II

Despite all that we have said thus far about facts, we have still not really said precisely what it is to be a fact. To do so, it is important to find out what phrases of the form 'the fact that $p$' mean. If we can define such phrases generally, we shall be in a good position to understand the ontological nature of facts and to explain the various facts about facts that were mentioned in the last section.[9]

---

[8] 'My being white' *can* refer to a fact, but that is not how we are using it here. Cf. p. 79f., above. Even 'my present whiteness' *can* be used to refer to a fact.

[9] If time permitted, I think it could be shown that ordinary use of the

Philosophers have long thought that facts bore a special relation to propositions and have held that of necessity there is such a thing as the fact that $p$ if and only if (and just as long as) the proposition that $p$ is true—to put the matter clearly but sloppily. Some philosophers have attempted both to acknowledge this special relation and to avoid locating facts in space by claiming that facts are true propositions. They have held, in effect, that for all appropriate true sentences $p$, ⌜the fact that $p$⌝ designates what ⌜the true proposition that $p$⌝ designates; and have seemed to hold that this codesignation obtains because of the very meaning of the expressions involved.[10] Thus they seem committed to saying that 'the fact that men now exist' and 'the true proposition that men now exist' mean the same and, for that very reason, are codesignative. And such a view seems natural, since it seems to be analytically true that there is such a thing as the fact that men now exist if and only if there is such a thing as the true proposition that men now exist.

I would not want to dispute this last claim of analyticity; but it does not entail the theory of facts just mentioned. My own view is that the fact that men now exist is just the *truth* (*being true*) of the proposition that men now exist, and that this identity is due to the fact that ⌜the fact that $p$⌝ means pretty much the same as ⌜the truth of the proposition that $p$⌝. This theory is perfectly compatible with the analyticity of the claim that there is such a thing as the fact that men now exist if and only if there is such a thing as the true proposition that men now exist. For clearly there is such a thing as the true proposition that men now exist if and only if there is such a thing as the truth of the proposition that men now exist, and this is as analytic as the claim that Mary's beauty exists as long as Mary is beauti-

phrases 'is a fact' and 'the facts' is too ambiguous, too non-referential, and/or too idiomatic to indicate much about the ontological status or nature of facts.

[10] See C. Ducasse, 'Propositions, Opinions, Sentences, and Facts', *J. Phil.* 37, 1940, pp. 701–11; A Woozley, *Theory of Knowledge*, London: Hutchinson, 1960, pp. 169–73.

ful, if it exists at all. On the view that facts are true propositions, facts are all necessary entities, presumably. But on the view I am proposing, if it is contingently true that $p$, then the truth of the proposition that $p$, and the fact that $p$, are not necessary entities. This is easily seen if one recalls our discussion of the existence conditions of states of affairs like the redness of Mary's hair, and also keeps in mind that 'the truth of the proposition that $p$' is a rigid designator. But what evidence can be brought forward in favour of saying that facts are truths of propositions and not true propositions?

Some of the most persuasive evidence, I think, comes from the existence of a large number of psychological, epistemic, and explanatory contexts where we can talk (fairly) idiomatically about facts and about the truth of certain propositions, but not about true propositions. I can be shocked, or disturbed, by the fact that $p$, and also by the truth of the proposition that $p$; but one cannot, without strangeness and incomprehension, say that one is shocked, or disturbed, by the true proposition that $p$. One can be surprised at a fact or at the truth of some proposition, but not at a true proposition—at least this is how we speak about these matters. What would it *mean* to say that one was surprised at a given true proposition: that one was surprised at its existence? Surely what we are in general surprised at is the proposition's *being true*, not its very existence, which is just what our theory suggests.

Other contexts also suggest how far our usage of phrases of the form 'the true proposition that $p$' is from our usage of phrases of the form 'the fact that $p$'. I can be aware of the fact that Harry is at home, but can I be aware of the *true proposition* that Harry is at home (except perhaps in the sense that I know that that proposition—which is in fact true whether I know it or not—exists, which is a different thing altogether)? I can, however, be aware of the *truth of* the proposition or claim that Harry is at home, and this is still further reason for thinking that ⌜the fact that $p$⌝ means pretty much the same as and is codesignative with ⌜the truth of the proposition that $p$⌝. In a similar vein, we can say 'All men are equal; the realization of that fact changed my life' and can say 'All men are equal; the realization of the truth of that proposition changed my life', but cannot with similar meaning say 'All men are equal; the realization of that true proposition changed my life'.

Various occurrences or states of affairs can also be due to (result from) certain facts. Someone might well say: All men are created equal; and it is solely due to that fact that dictatorships are always eventually overthrown or destroyed. And in a similar way, one might well say: All men are created equal, and it is solely due to the truth of that proposition that dictatorships never last. But no one would ever say that the failure of various dictatorships was due to the *true proposition* that all men are created equal. For nothing can result from or be due to (the existence of) a necessarily existent proposition. In the light of all the above examples, therefore, I think it should seem somewhat implausible to claim that facts are (by virtue of the very meaning of 'fact') identical with true propositions. There is some reason, however, to think that in most contexts phrases of the form 'the fact that $p$' are replaceable (without change of meaning) by phrases of the form 'the truth of the proposition that $p$'. And this supports our view that any given fact is the truth of some corresponding proposition, and that this is analytic of what it is to be a fact.

# III

We have argued for the superiority of our theory that for all appropriate true sentences $p$ ⌜the fact that $p$⌝ is synonymous with, and thus analytically codesignative with, ⌜the truth of the proposition that $p$⌝ to *other* theories about the identity of facts and the meaning of fact talk. But our theory also recommends itself for its ability to explain the facts about facts that we discussed in section one of the present chapter. For example, facts cannot come back into existence; and if we think of any fact as the truth of some proposition, it should be clear why facts cannot come back into existence. For the truth of a proposition can only come back into existence if the proposition is at one time false and then later true. And this is clearly impossible on contemporary philosophical usage of the term 'proposition'. Of course, Mary's unhappiness may come back into existence, but that is because a person can be alternatingly happy and unhappy in a way that a proposition cannot alternate between falsehood and truth.

We argued earlier that all facts are either (a) essentially unceasing or (b) such that if they exist at some $t$, they essentially exist only at $t$. Any entity meeting either of (a) or (b)—which are definable solely in terms of our primitives—is what we can call a *temporally bound* entity. Facts are not the only kind of entities that are temporally bound. Necessarily existent entities like propositions count as temporally bound—assuming that they exist at all. Times, if they exist, will presumably meet condition (b) and thus also qualify as temporally bound. Our definition of temporal boundness sets no conditions on the coming into being of entities. One reason for this is that the conditions for the coming into being of facts are by no means obvious, in the light of Aristotle's problem of future contingencies. If, as Aristotle seems to have held, propositions about as yet (causally) undetermined events, etc., in the future do not have truth value, then there will not now be any facts about such events, etc., and it will, presumably, sometimes be a logically contingent matter *when* a given fact about the future, or a given tenseless fact concerning the whole infinity of time, will come into being. Though I am inclined to disagree with Aristotle, I shall not press the matter. The coming into being of facts *may* be no more rigidly determined than that of the sorts of states of affairs discussed in Chapter 5. But we can, in any case, distinguish facts from such states of affairs in terms of the rigidity of the conditions of their perishing or continuing to be, or, more precisely, in terms of temporal boundness as we have specified it. Facts are one and all temporally bound, but such states of affairs as Helen's beauty, the enmity between

China and Russia, there being ravens, and Helen's present looks are one and all not temporally bound.

At the beginning of this chapter, I said that there seemed to be less reason to attempt to assign a location to facts than to do so with respect to states of affairs of the kind discussed in Chapter 5. We can now understand something of why this is so. An unbound (i.e., not temporally bound) state of affairs like Helen's beauty logically depends on Helen and so it is not unnatural to locate it where Helen is, just as thoughts are sometimes said to be located in the brain, on which they causally depend. Facts like Helen's being beautiful at $t$ (where '$t$' is a constant) do not, however, depend on Helen, since they can exist even when Helen no longer does. And so there is less reason to locate such facts in or around Helen in particular. If such facts are anywhere, they are in the world, the universe, in general, not in some particular places as opposed to others. And perhaps all it means to say that such facts are in the world is just that certain propositions are true of, or true in, the world.

One thing I am inclined to say about facts is that they cannot alter over time. But, of course, we argued above, in Chapter 5, that certain of the kinds of states of affairs we discussed there *could* undergo alteration. I think we can use our view of facts to explain this difference. Helen can be beautiful in different ways at different times, so it is not unnatural to think that Helen's beauty can alter over time. But Helen cannot be beautiful at $t$ in different ways at different times. It cannot be the case that yesterday Helen is beautiful$_m$ at $t$, but today she is beautiful$_n$ at $t$. And so because a time element is already built into Helen's being beautiful at $t$ in the particular way it is, there is no room left for Helen's being beautiful at $t$ to undergo alteration over time. Thus facts seem to be incapable of altering.

Our definition of $\ulcorner$(is) the fact that $p\urcorner$ is not by essence and accident and involves notions other than our primitives.[11] It

[11] There seems to be an epistemic sense of 'fact' in which facts contrast with theories or hypotheses and in which appropriate talk about the fact that $p$ implies that it is known that $p$. But since it also makes sense to

thus stands outside our system of definitions framed in terms of or ultimately frameable in terms of our exiguous stock of primitive notions or notion-clusters. But our definition of what it is to be a fact can benefit our system of definitions by enabling us to see where some of those definitions are inaccurate and how they can be repaired. Consider, for example, our earlier recommendations about the definition of 'is a change'. (See pp. 21, 33f.) If we had spelled out that earlier definition in its entirety, it would have read:

'is a change' means about the same as 'is essentially: existent only if something other than a time moves or alters or comes into being or goes out of existence; and is such that it is not possible that for all $t$ and $t'$ when it exists, there is something exactly like it between and/or at $t$ and $t'$ that is not essentially: existent only if something other than a time moves or alters or comes into being or goes out of existence'.

Given what we have said about facts and about time previously, it may be that for any possible entity that exists at some time, it is necessary that there exist some tensed fact involving that entity. It may be, for example, that I essentially exist only if there is *some* tensed fact *like* that fact that I now exist. As far as we have shown, furthermore, such facts may essentially go out of existence with the passage of time and the passage of time, even without change, may be logically or metaphysically necessary. In that case, it may well be that I, and every possible entity exactly like me, essentially: exist only if something other than a time, namely, a tensed fact, goes out of existence. And the same may be true of every other (temporal) entity in the universe.

This problem with our earlier definition of 'is a change' can be dealt with by replacing the occurrence of 'other than a time'

speak of facts of which everyone is ignorant, I think there is a non-epistemic sense of 'the fact that $p$' relevant to metaphysics, and this is the sense, as I have argued here, in which to be a fact is to be the truth of some proposition.

in it by the phrase 'other than a temporally bound entity'. But problems remain. Consider the fact that wars begin. This fact essentially: exists only if something other than a temporally bound entity comes into existence, namely, some war or other. But we would not, presumably, want to call the fact that wars begin a change (or event), even if we do consider wars changes (or events); so our definition of 'is a change' is still inadequate. This kind of problem can, however, be easily dealt with in terms of the difference between facts and other entities. Facts appear to be the only counterexamples to our current definition of change, so why not complete our definition by making it read:

> *'is a change' means approximately the same as 'is a non-temporally-bound entity that is essentially: existent only if something other than a temporally bound entity moves or alters or comes into being or goes out of existence; and that is such that it is not possible that for all $t$ and $t'$ when it exists, there is something exactly like it between and/or at $t$ and $t'$ that is not essentially: existent only if something other than a temporally bound entity moves or alters or comes into being or goes out of existence'.

The same problem we have just been dealing with also yields difficulties for our previous definitions of what it is to be an alteration and what it is to be a motion (or movement). (See p. 33f., above.) Various facts are not themselves motions or alterations, but could not exist unless something not temporally bound moved or altered, etc. Again, we can handle such problems by ruling out all temporally bound entities as alterations or motions in our definitions of those concepts. And this can be done by prefacing those definitions by 'is a non-temporally-bound entity such that' or some similar locution.[12] Our final definition of 'is an alteration' should then read:

[12] The notion of temporal boundness as defined above seems a natural way to distinguish facts from other entities. But our use of that notion in defining change threatens our whole system of definitions with circularity. For the idea of temporal boundness involves the idea of going out of

*'is an alteration' means approximately the same as 'is a non-temporally-bound entity $x$ such that $x$ essentially exists only if something alters and such that it is not possible that for all $t$ and $t'$ when $x$ exists, there is something $y$ not identical with $x$ that is exactly like $x$ between and/or at $t$ and $t'$ and that is not essentially existent only if something alters'.

Our final definition of 'is a motion (or movement)' should, in like fashion, read:

*'is a motion (or movement)' means approximately the same as 'is a non-temporally-bound entity $x$ such that $x$ essentially exists only if something moves and such that it is not possible that for all $t$ and $t'$ when $x$ exists, there is something $y$ not identical with $x$ that is exactly like $x$ between and/or at $t$ and $t'$ and that is not essentially existent only if something moves'.

At this point, it might be wondered whether our definitions of alteration, motion and change do not rule out certain instantaneous alterations, motions, or events. For if they do,

existence and thus the notion of the future; and our definition of the future used the notion of a physical body, which, as we shall define it, involves the notion of a change, as well as that of temporal boundness. In order to complete our system of definitions by essence and accident using only five (and later, I hope, only three) primitives as our ultimate building blocks, we must avoid this kind of circle. The best way of doing so, I think, is to specify a notion of temporal boundness capable of distinguishing facts from other entities in the way we need to do *without implicitly involving the idea of the future*. For purposes of system and absolute accuracy, then, we should perhaps say that something is temporally bound just in case it is such that if it exists at some $t$, it essentially exists only at $t$, or else is such that there cannot be something $y$ exactly like it at some time and a $t'$ and $t''$ such that all times when $y$ exists are between $t'$ and $t''$, and identical with neither $t'$ nor $t''$. Such a definition of temporal boundness is more cumbersome than our earlier one, but enables us to avoid circularity, I think. For most of our purposes, however, temporal boundness can be understood loosely, as defined in the text above. In the light of these problems, moreover, certain minor alterations not worth discussing also need to be made in our definitions.

then those definitions are surely too strong. Consider a particular instant colour change that occurs in a given leaf. Is such an entity a temporally bound entity that is not accounted an alteration or change by our final definitions of those notions? I think not. Such instantaneous events, changes, etc., may essentially not exist at more than one time, but it does not follow that if they exist at some *t*, they essentially exist at no time other than *t*. They might have existed at some earlier or later single moment. If, as common sense would seem to dictate, the Second World War did not essentially begin (to exist) at that moment when it first began, why should this not also be true of instantaneous events, changes, etc.? If we individuate events in terms of their particular (causal) origins, why would it not be possible for an instant event that in fact was brought about by factors *a*, *b*, and *c* to have been brought about earlier by the earlier operation of those same factors? I can think of no reason, then, to think of instant events, etc., as temporally bound, and our present definitions of alteration and change can, I think, stand.[13]

I would like, at this point, to answer what seems to me to be interesting challenge to the theory of facts we have presented.[14] We noted in Chapter 5 that such phrases as 'Helen's beauty' can mean either 'Helen's being beautiful' or 'the fact that Helen is beautiful'. Given this ambiguity, 'Helen's beauty' can refer to either of two different kinds of entities: a non-temporally-bound state of affairs and a temporally bound fact. But then why not hold that 'the truth of the proposition that men now exist', for example, is ambiguous and can refer to either of two sorts of entities? Either that phrase means 'the fact that the proposition that men now exist is true' or it means 'the-proposition-that-

---

[13] Given our modifications of our definitions of change, motion, and alteration, our definition of eventhood need not be altered verbally. I have not taken the time to modify our definition of processhood in the light of the problems raised by facts, but this could be done in much the same way we modified others of our definitions just above.

[14] I am indebted for this challenge to Saul Kripke.

men-now-exist-being-true'. In the former case, of course, one is referring to a fact, perhaps even to the fact that men now exist, for the fact that men now exist might well be the same fact as the fact that the proposition that men now exist is true. But if we understand 'the truth of the proposition that men now exist' in this way, there is nothing startling or interesting about the fact (if it is a fact) that the phrase refers to a fact and is coreferential with 'the fact that men now exist', nothing that we did not already (implicitly) know in knowing that 'Helen's beauty' can be coreferential with 'the fact that Helen is beautiful'.

What would be interesting would be if 'the-proposition-that-men-now-exist-being-true' referred to a fact in a way that 'Helen's being beautiful' does not. And I think this is the case. Helen's being beautiful is clearly not a fact because it is a state of affairs that is not temporally bound. But the-proposition-that-men-now-exist-being-true is temporally bound; for that state of affairs (once it exists) can go out of existence only when the proposition that men now exist goes out of existence, since a proposition cannot, once true, become false or untrue. And that state of affairs also cannot exist at a time when the proposition that men now exist does not. Since the proposition that men now exist either cannot cease to exist or exists at a time $t$ such that it essentially exists at no time other than $t$ (exists only at $t$), this will also have to be true of the-proposition-that-men-now-exist-being-true, in which case that state of affairs will be temporally bound. Thus 'Helen's beauty', when understood as meaning 'Helen's being beautiful' does not (typically) refer to a temporally bound entity or fact; but 'the truth of the proposition that men now exist', when interpreted to mean 'the-proposition-that-men-now-exist-being-true', does refer to a temporally bound state of affairs, and that state of affairs, I want to hold, is precisely the fact that men now exist. This is, moreover, a far more informative and controversial claim than the fact that men now exist is identical with the fact that the proposition that men now exist is true.

It should be pointed out, finally, that on our theory, there can be 'negative' facts (i.e., facts corresponding to propositions most people would *call* negative), as well as 'universal' or 'general' facts. I think the only reason why some philosophers have denied the existence of such facts has been their conviction that facts are definite and (usually) spatially bounded entities out in the world that *make* propositions true.[15] But we have argued against such a view. Facts do not seem to be spatially located in specific places the way material objects, and even some temporally unbound states of affairs are. Nor do they *cause* or *create* the truth of propositions; rather they *constitute* the truth of propositions. And (loosely speaking)[16] propositions *can* be 'universal' or 'negative'.[17]

[15] E.g., B. Berofsky in 'Causality and General Laws' (*J. Phil.* 63, 1966, p. 153) seems to hold that facts are what make propositions, or what have you, true.

[16] I am wary about talking about universal or negative propositions, because universality and negativeness do not seem to be absolute properties of propositions, etc. Universality and negativeness seem to be relative to language or to certain initial assumptions or starting points. On this see Frege's 'Negation' in Geach and Black, eds., *The Philosophical Writings of Gottlob Frege*, Oxford: 1966, p. 125f.

[17] The theory of facts presented here also commits one to speaking of mathematical facts, but I do not think this really involves any stretching of usage. Surely, it is perfectly natural to speak of ignoring or forgetting the fact that 51 is composite (not prime).

# 7. Physical Bodies

In the present chapter, I shall attempt to define the notion of a physical body by essence and accident, making use only of our five primitive notion-clusters, or of notions that we have defined in terms of them. In Chapters 4 and 5, I provided this kind of definition of the notion of a physical entity. But this definition is insufficient to define the narrower notion of a physical body. For there are all sorts of (possible or putative) physical entities that are not physical bodies: surfaces of physical bodies, (groups of) points on or in physical bodies, physical monads with location but no dimensions, aspects of (states of affairs involving) physical bodies (or other physical entities), Minkowski space-time 'worms' of physical bodies (or other physical entities), and physical laws or necessities—not to mention duos, trios, classes, etc., of various entities of the kinds just mentioned. The main task here will be to find modal predicates or properties in terms of which we can distinguish all the above sorts of entities from physical bodies.

## I

Before I put forward a definition of physical bodyhood, I would like briefly to consider various other (to my mind inadequate) views that have been or could be advocated about the nature of physical bodies and the way the notion of a physical body should be defined.

In the *Categories*, Chapter 5, Aristotle says that the most distinctive mark of substance is its ability to admit of contraries, i.e., to undergo alteration. And it has often been thought to be a distinctive trait of physical *objects* or physical *bodies*[1] that they can continue to exist despite the diversity implied in alteration over time. Unfortunately, the ability to alter cannot be definitive of physical bodyhood, since many other putative physical entites can alter too: physical monads, surfaces of bodies, the stuff of which one or another body is composed, and—if what we said in Chapter 5 was correct—aspects of bodies and kinds of bodies as well.

In *Some Main Problems of Philosophy*,[2] G. E. Moore defines the notion of a material object as being the notion of something that occupies (a volume of) space, and is not a sense datum, a mind, or an act of consciousness. But this definition seems to be met by various putative physical entities that are neither material objects nor physical bodies. The physical kind or type of thing piano seems to occupy a certain voluminous portion of the world and is no sense datum, etc. Similarly, the gold in a given ring meets Moore's definition, but is not, like the ring itself, a physical body or material object. So Moore's definition includes too much, either as a definition of material objecthood or as a definition of the broader notion of a physical body.

It might be tempting to think the basically Aristotelian thought that physical bodies are those physical entities that are somehow (ontologically) independent (of other physical entities), capable of existing apart from other physical entities. But the trouble is that physical bodies do depend on other possible or putative physical entities. A given table depends, for its existence, on the state of affairs there being physical bodies, as well as on (the existence of) matter in general. Nor could we refine things slightly and successfully define physical bodyhood by saying that a physical body is something not depending on anything (partly) exterior to it, for matter can be partly exterior

---

[1] Physical objects are all physical bodies; but not vice versa. A body of gas is, I think, not really an *object* in the ordinary sense of the word. I am interested here in defining the more general and pervasive (possibly somewhat technical) notion of a physical *body*.

[2] P. 131.

to a given physical body. And it does not help at all to define a physical body as something not depending on anything *totally* exterior to it, for if this is true of physical bodies, it may well also be true of various kinds of bodies and aspects of bodies.[3]

At this point, it might occur to one to say that there cannot be a correct definition of physical bodyhood, because physical bodies do not constitute a unitary kind of thing, i.e., because there is nothing (interesting) common to all and only physical bodies, but at best only family resemblances among them. Such views have been held by several philosophers in recent times. In *Sense and Sensibilia*,[4] Austin suggests that there is no such *kind* of thing as material objects (and so, presumably, a fortiori, no such *kind* of thing as physical bodies).[5] More recently, J. Pollock has suggested that the notion of a physical or material object is indefinable,[6] and, presumably, he would say the same about the notion of a physical body.

Perhaps these views are correct; but it seems to me intuitively that there is something common to physical bodies in virtue of which they count as physical bodies *rather than* as surfaces of bodies, aspects of bodies, pairs of bodies, and the like; there seems on the face of it to be something (however hard it is to state) about bodies that makes them different from these other kinds of physical entities. And if we can give a plausible definition of physical bodyhood by essence and accident via our primitives, perhaps that will undermine or tend to undermine the view that physical bodies have nothing in common and are not a unitary, definable kind of entity.

[3] To define physical bodies as being physical entities that underlie, or are the substrata of, qualities is no help either. How can anything that exists fail to be a substratum of qualities in any straightforward and readily understandable sense of that expression?

[4] Oxford: Clarendon, 1962, pp. 8, 14.

[5] A similar view is advocated by A. Lazerowitz in 'Moore's "Proof of an External World"', in Schilpp, ed., *The Philosophy of G. E. Moore*, N.Y.: Tudor, 1952, p. 405f.

[6] In 'Criteria and Our Knowledge of the Material World', *Phil. Review* 76, 1967, pp. 28–60.

## II

At the beginning of this chapter we mentioned various of the sorts of physical entities that there are (or may be) that are not physical bodies. In order to define physical bodyhood, let us try to distinguish all such entities from physical bodies, via our five primitives.

Some of the kinds of entities mentioned at the beginning of the chapter are easily ruled out by conditions of physical bodyhood statable via our primitives. Surfaces of bodies and (groups of) points on or in bodies, for example, can sometimes be three-dimensional, inasmuch as a given surface or group of points may not be 'flat' or lie in a single plane. But such a surface or group of points surely cannot occupy a volume of space, have volume. And physical bodies are all voluminous. A physical monad, if such a thing is possible, is not a body just because such a thing is not extended, much less voluminous. So surfaces, (groups of) points, and physical monads can easily be ruled out by a definition of physical bodyhood into which is built the claim that:

(a) of necessity anything $x$ is a physical body only if $x$ is physical and a non-change and occupies a volume of space (is voluminous).

Next consider space-time worms. If the space-time worm of a given table is thought of as an entity not identical with the table itself, it must be because the space-time worm of a table has time built into it in a way that tables do not. Tables can come into being, perish, alter and move. But there is no second or deeper time for a four-dimensional space-time entity like a space-time worm to perish, alter, etc., in. It is not the kind of entity that can perish, alter, etc. There may be 'bends and ends' to space-time worms corresponding to where the objects of which they are the worms moved or perished, etc., but the worms themselves do not, as four-dimensional entities, do any of these things. In this degree space-time worms are like, perhaps are even identical with, the (complete) histories of objects or of other entities. For the history of a given object, once one conceives there to be such a thing *in its entirety*, is not the kind of thing one thinks of as altering, moving, perishing, etc.

To eliminate space-time worms of physical bodies or entities, by our definitional conditions of physical bodyhood, we can add to condition (a) the condition that:

(b) of necessity anything $x$ is a physical body only if $x$ is mutable (can alter), can move, and is not temporally bound.

Appropriately enough, our just-introduced condition (b) also rules out immutable aspects of physical things—e.g., the present state of my body—from counting as physical bodies.[7]

We must now distinguish between natural laws governing (or

[7] Though worms and states of bodies, or of other things, are both immutable, they differ greatly with respect to the notion of exact likeness. A given worm could have been otherwise than it in fact is, if the body, say, of which it is the worm had been otherwise. But the present state of a given body is not something that could have been otherwise than it in fact is, and indeed it would not have existed if that body had always been otherwise than it in fact now is. Of course, even then there could have been *such a thing* as the present state of that body, but that state would not have been the particular state that body in fact is in now. (This illustrates the fact that 'the present state of that body' is never a rigid designator.) Of course, 'the present state of that body could have been otherwise' can be true when it is understood to mean 'there could at present have been a state of that body that was unlike the state that body is actually in at present'; I am simply saying that it is false when understood as meaning: 'the present state of that body is not essentially as it is'.

The idea that some things could have been otherwise, even though they are immutable, can be fairly well approximated using our primitives. What is true of worm $a$, but not of state $b$, of a given body is that there is an $x$ identical with it such that it is possible for there to be a $y$ that is only accidentally not exactly like $x$. It seems that anything that can alter could have been otherwise, but not, as we have seen, vice versa.

about) the physical and physical bodies, and build that distinction into our definition of physical bodyhood, if we have not already done so. There are many different views about what natural laws are. Sometimes it is said that laws are lawlike true sentence tokens or sentence types. Sentence tokens are sometimes just events of sound emission, sometimes physical inscriptions. The former are changes and so are ruled out by condition (a) above. The latter may well count as physical bodies and not need to be eliminated by our definition. If laws are sentence types, then perhaps they are immutable or temporally bound platonic entities and already eliminated by condition (b). But I am somewhat inclined to think that sentence types are (physical) kinds, or species, of sentence tokens,[8] and if that is true, then they are not, I think, eliminated by (a) and (b). However, such entities will be eliminated below when I shall state a condition of physical bodyhood that eliminates *all* physical kinds, so we can forget about sentence types at this point.

Laws are often thought of as propositions maintained (in a certain way) by one or another scientific discipline, rather than as sentences. But laws thus conceived are temporally bound platonic entities that are already eliminated by condition (b). There is, however, yet another sense of 'law', one that has been almost completely neglected by recent philosophers and in which what is a law in no way depends on the having of empirical evidence for or epistemic attitudes towards various sentences or propositions (of science). The existence of such a further sense of 'natural law' can be shown as follows.

We can certainly, without oddness, say: 'there would have been natural or physical laws, even if there never had been any science of physics'. But note the strangeness of: 'there would

[8] I am surer that word-types are non-platonic species of word-tokens than that sentence-types are non-platonic species of sentence tokens, because, for one thing, it seems more natural to say that there are (infinitely many) English *sentences* that will never be used, than to say that there are (infinitely many) English *words* that will never be used.

have been laws of physics, even if there had never been any science of physics'. The explanation of this difference in what it is natural to say lies, I believe, in the fact that 'law of physics' typically means something like 'lawlike (true) proposition (or sentence) that physics subscribes to', whereas 'physical law' and 'natural law' often mean something different, in such a way that something can be a natural or physical law even if there never is any science. Natural laws, in this latter sense, are, I think, natural necessities; and there can be such necessities independently of the existence of any science or human knowledge. That natural or physical laws (of the kind) that are natural or physical necessities are not sentences or propositions, furthermore, is evidenced by the fact that we can quite naturally say that in our universe certain natural laws (natural necessities) prevent there being (make it impossible for there to be) a perpetual motion machine, but would not say that certain lawlike true sentences or propositions prevent such things from existing, since propositions are platonic and (presumably) essentially uncausative, and sentences are either platonic and uncausative or else fairly puny. Thus I think there is a sense of 'law' in which laws are non-sentential, non-propositional necessities or laws in nature.[9] The question then arises whether any conditions of physical bodyhood already presented, or capable of being formulated in terms of our primitives, can be used to eliminate laws that are natural or physical necessities from counting as physical bodies, on our definition. To answer this question, we must consider further what sorts of entities natural necessities are. Consider the natural necessity (assuming that it is a natural necessity) that all bodies attract one another. Is this not really just the natural necessity (its being naturally necessary) that at all times and places all bodies attract one another? If so, then laws that are natural or physical necessities

[9] 'Law of nature' is used more of natural necessities than of lawlike propositions, because we cannot understand 'law of nature' as 'law of the discipline nature' the way we can understand 'law of physics' to mean 'law of the discipline physics'.

would seem to be temporally bound entities that are already ruled out by our condition (b) of physical bodyhood. One might even think, in addition, that the natural necessity that at all times and places all bodies attract one another is identical with the *fact* that it is naturally necessary that at all times and places all bodies attract one another—since the latter is also temporally bound and is in various other ways ontologically similar to the natural necessity that at all times and places all bodies attract one another. And clearly our definition already rules out facts as counting as physical bodies.

However, one might wonder whether all laws that are natural necessities are or need to be temporally bound. Could there not, one might ask, be a natural necessity capable of ceasing to exist; is it not possible for the laws in the universe to change (in the sense of ceasing to exist and being replaced by other laws)? Such possibilities are ruled out or ignored by most philosophers of science; but some philosophers of science have seemed willing to grant the possibility of such perishing and replacement of laws.[10] This idea is an intriguing one; but the more I have attempted to work out the implications of law replacement, the more incoherent the idea has seemed to me. If one assumes that laws can cease to be, there seem to be insuperable problems in understanding or explaining how or why laws (of that sort) have gone out of existence and how or why laws (of that sort) have stayed in existence. I shall not attempt to go into these difficulties any further here, but I shall assume, as most philosophers and scientists indeed always have, that laws (natural necessities) cannot cease to be, but rather are built into the (structure of the) universe in something like the way that tenseless facts are—even if laws are not identical with any such facts. Furthermore, even if there are or can be temporally unbound laws of the sort that have sometimes been supposed to

[10] See E. Nagel, *The Structure of Science*, N.Y.: Harcourt, Brace and World, 1961, pp. 378–80; Planck, *The Universe in the Light of Modern Physics*, 1931, p. 63; and Poincaré, 'The Evolution of Laws' in *Mathematics and Science: Last Essays*, N.Y.: Dover, 1963, pp. 1–14.

exist or to be possible, I think the conditions in terms of which we shall ultimately be defining the notion of a physical body will suffice to rule out temporally unbound laws (or classes, duos, etc., of such).

Let us then continue our attempt to define the notion of a physical body. Consider physical duos like the duo of (table) *a* and (table) *b*. Such a duo depends on each of its members and neither of the members (logically) can exist even partly outside that duo while the duo exists. Bodies, on the other hand, do not, I think, depend on anything else that cannot to any degree be outside them while they exist. A body *a* may depend on the race (class) of things identical with body *a* or body *b*, and if *b* does not exist, then *a* depends on something (other than itself) that is in no way exterior to it. But if *b* could exist, then the race of things identical with *a* or *b* could be to some degree exterior to *a* even though *a* depended on it. I am inclined to think, indeed, that:

(c) of necessity anything *x* is a physical body only if *x* does not and cannot depend on any (physical) entity other than *x* that cannot be in any way exterior to *x* while *x* exists.

This condition (c) eliminates all duos (pairs), trios, quartets, etc., of physical bodies, without eliminating physical bodies themselves. However, the assumption that (c) does not eliminate physical bodies depends on another assumption that should now be made explicit, the assumption, namely, that physical bodies do not (and cannot) depend on any of their physical bodily parts. For if bodies can depend on their bodily parts, then they may well depend on something (else) physical that cannot exist even to some degree outside them while they exist, and thus fail condition (c).

I should like, however, to suggest two lines of argument for the view that physical bodies do not logically depend on any bodies that are parts of themselves, or, indeed, therefore, on any other physical bodies whatsoever. One line of argument is based

9

on considerations of how much of a given object we can take away before having to think of the object as having perished, ceased to exist. And let us, for brevity and simplicity's sake, concentrate only on homogeneous objects, objects all of whose parts of any given size are equally important to its survival.[11] With respect to such objects, I think that preservation of two-thirds of an original object is clearly sufficient for the survival of the original object, and that preservation of only one-third of the original object is insufficient for its survival. Anywhere in between, the question of survival is either indeterminate or very hard to answer. Let us, then, consider a thing $b$, and its parts $c$, $d$, and $e$.

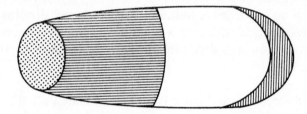

$b$ is the whole of the above-illustrated object, $c$ is the dotted part of it, $d$ the part consisting of $c$ and the part with horizontal stripes, and $e$ is the part that consists of $d$ and the blank part. $b$ is clearly capable of existing without $c$, since $c$ is less than one-third of $b$ in size. And $b$ is not, I think, in any clear-cut way dependent on $d$, which is about half the size of $b$. But one might think that in any case, $b$ depends on $e$, which takes up two-thirds of it. But is this so? Let us imagine two-thirds of $e$ destroyed; still *more* than one-third of $b$ would remain (or could remain), since there are parts of $b$ that are not parts of

[11] Obviously in actual fact some parts of some objects are of greater importance to their survival than equally large and voluminous other parts. The torso of a statue seems to be more important to its survival than the sum of both its arms and one of its legs, which could weigh just as much as the torso and take up just as much room.

*e*. And in that case, again, it would be by no means clear that *b* did not still exist, or thus that *b* depended on *e*.

What this brief argument tends to show, I think, is that bodies do not definitely depend on any of their bodily parts. Even if two-thirds and one-third are the wrong fractions, and even if the penumbral area of cases where the question of survival has no definite answer, and is not just hard to answer, is differently located, as far as fractions of the original object are concerned, or is much smaller than we have said, it should be clear in the light of the above argument that it will still not be possible to find cases of homogeneous bodies definitely depending on any (one) of their bodily parts, or, thus, indeed, on any other bodies whatsoever. The argument requires complication in order to be extended to heterogeneous objects, but it should be fairly clear that such an argument would just be a complex extension of the argument given above, and I shall not go into its details here.

What also tend to show that physical bodies depend on none of their parts are certain facts about the way objects (logically) can persist through enormous and radical alteration. Consider, for example, a shoe that alters of its own accord in a lawful and orderly way as follows. The shoe slowly turns into a longer shoe and then slowly back into a shoe of the same size as the shoe was originally and exactly like the shoe as it originally was; then the shoe gradually changes back into a longer shoe, then develops some metal in its tip, then changes back into a long shoe without metal, and finally shrinks back to its original size. Again the shoe starts changing. This time it gets longer, develops metal at its tip, which then shapes itself into the shape of a hammer's head, and then it goes through those changes in reverse order until it is finally again a shoe of the sort it originally was. Let us imagine that the (thing that is originally a) shoe continues to go through cyclical alterations like those described just above and that each new time the shoe goes through a process of cyclical alteration, it gets to be more unlike the original shoe than it got to be during the previous cycle—in the manner we described just above. Can we not imagine, then, that the shoe, in an orderly and lawful way, eventually goes through a cycle of alteration during the course of which it becomes (very much like) a stuffed owl, and at the end of which it returns to its original shoe state? If we were to witness or learn about such 'behaviour', would we not be inclined to think of the object originally there, a shoe of a certain size, as going through various stages in which it become successively a this, a that, and another thing, and as existing again as it was originally, at the end of each cycle of such stages? If such altera- tion occurred in the manner I described, we would, I think, consider that alteration to be the enormous and radical altera- tion of a single thing; and two factors favouring such a view are the orderliness of the alterations and their reversibility.[12]

If all this is so, then a given thing that is a shoe need not depend on any given one of its parts. It need not, for example, depend on its tongue, or on its sole, because it can organize its own lawful and reversible cycles of alteration through stages in which it is (much like) a stuffed owl and in which its tongue, or its sole, no longer exists. For in such cases, I believe we think of the whole, which organizes and orders the radical changes that occur, as persisting, but not the parts, which do not, presumably, organize (all) the alterations and which are 'sacrificed' temporarily by the whole as a means to its radical alterations.[13] (So I am saying that it is in part the fact that the thing that is a shoe organizes its own alterations, rather than

---

[12] Orderliness of alteration is clearly a factor commonly thought of as favouring the claim that a given entity has survived some radical alteration; it is a factor, for example, in our thinking of a butterfly as an animal that was once a caterpillar. Reversibility too has weight sometimes. A man whose heart has stopped may still be thought of as existing (not dead), if we think we can start it beating again, but presumably not if we think the beating cannot be started up again.

[13] This whole way of seeing things goes against Kripke's view (in 'Naming and Necessity', footnote 57) that given tables are essentially tables.

having them imposed from without, that enables it to survive huge change.)[14]

Nor do I think that the above possibilities of radical alteration exist only for shoes and other objects that *might have* existed but in fact do not. As things now stand, of course, it would be physically impossible for the shoes, etc., that actually exist to alter in the orderly way described above. But this seems to me to be only accidentally true of those shoes, etc., that now exist in the world. I have just named the shoe on my right foot 'Harry'. It seems to me to be logically possible that Harry should begin (or have begun) to alter in ways it has (had) never done before, and, indeed, in ways that it is in fact *physically* impossible for things (and thus Harry) to alter. The world, in other words, obeys certain physical or natural laws, but could have obeyed different laws. And I cannot see why the things that in fact exist essentially exist in a world with precisely the laws our world contains. It is, for example, a law of the actual universe that shoes of such and such description at no time or place ever gradually alter in such a way as to become like stuffed owls. But why could it not have been a law, instead, that until the year 2000 (or, better, until the existence of a certain kind of distribution of matter-energy in the universe that, in fact, will first exist in the year 2000), no shoe anywhere can become like a stuffed owl, etc., but also a law that all shoes everywhere should start becoming like stuffed owls, etc., after the year 2000 (or after the appropriate matter-energy distribution existed)? But since such laws, in effect, only make a difference to the way(s)

[14] One reason, I think, why we believe that our bodies last throughout lifetimes, even though all, or most, of the cells in a body at a given time do not exist in it seven years later, is that this (constant) replacement of cells is organized by the body itself and is the means by which the body insures the continuation of a body and organs and cells of certain kinds. This is different from the case where a sock is darned and redarned until none of the original material is left. Because a sock does *not* organize the replacement of the material or stuff in it, the case of a darned and redarned sock is a less clear case of persistence on the part of an entity than is the case where a body organizes the steady replacement of its own cells.

things are and are changing after the year 2000, the existence of such laws does not seem to be incompatible with the existence of those objects, like Harry, that have in fact existed before the year 2000, but does entail that if such objects continue to exist after the year 2000, they will start to become like stuffed owls, etc., in a way that the laws of the actual world render impossible. Thus it does in the end seem to be logically possible even for such actually existent things as Harry to alter in the radical ways described earlier,[15] so we have another reason to think that even actually existing shoes, etc., do not depend on any of their parts that are physical bodies, or indeed on *any* physical bodies other than themselves. In that case, there is good reason to think that bodies meet condition (c) in a way that physical duos, trios, etc., do not. Furthermore, it would seem that aspects of (states of affairs involving) given bodies also fail to meet (c), since, for example, body $a$'s weighing, as a whole, three pounds (or $a$'s being larger than the sun) depends on something other than itself, namely, body $a$, that cannot exist in any way outside it while it exists. For what would it mean for a body to be in any way or degree spatially exterior to the state of affairs consisting in its weighing three pounds?

Condition (c) does not, however, suffice to enable us to define physical bodyhood, because various classes or species of physical entities also seem to meet (c). As far as I can tell, such classes or kinds as the class of things identical with body $a$ or body $b$ (or, if one prefers, the state of affairs: there being something identical with either $a$ or $b$) and the kind piano meet all the conditions we have formulated thus far without being physical

[15] What also favours the view that Harry, $et\,al.$, can alter in such radical ways is our (common-sense) belief in the logical possibility of forms of enchantment or bewitchment that we also believe not to be physically possible. We tend to think that it is imaginable, conceivable, with respect to our actually existing friends, or enemies, that they should become enchanted in story-book ways, even though we are sure that such enchantment is physically impossible, given the laws that actually exist in the universe. Furthermore, all the particles in actual objects can be imagined to 'freeze', stop their motion, but such a thing is physically impossible.

bodies. But such classes can be eliminated as follows. Let us use the term 'physical near-body' in such a way that it applies to just those things that meet conditions (a), (b), and (c). Physical bodies and the classes (kinds) just mentioned count as physical near-bodies. But the just-mentioned classes (kinds) are physical near-bodies that are essentially such as to be depended on by other physical near-bodies. The class of $a$ or $b$ cannot fail to be depended on by one of $a$ or $b$. And the kind piano cannot fail to be depended on by some more specific piano kind (like the kind heavy piano). On the other hand, physical bodies need not be depended on by other physical near-bodies; and so to eliminate the above-mentioned classes (kinds) and others like them, we need only say that:

(d) of necessity anything $x$ is a physical body only if $x$ is not essentially such as to be depended on by some physical near-body other than itself.

Our conditions (a) through (d) of physical bodyhood seem still to be insufficient to define that notion, because of certain problems presented by instances or samples of certain substances, in the modern English sense of 'substance'. Gold and silver are substances in this sense that seem pretty clearly to be ruled out by condition (d). But consider the gold in a given ring. That gold might well meet all the conditions we have mentioned up till now. For notice that the gold in a given ring can outlast (and does not depend on) the ring itself, just as the ring can presumably outlast the gold in it by turning to copper. Note too that the gold in a given ring no more depends on some part of the gold in that ring than a physical body depends on any of its bodily parts.

To complete our definition, then, we must find some distinction between physical bodies, on the one hand, and the stuff of which such bodies are composed, on the other, that can be formulated via our primitives. And the following may well constitute such a difference. A ring composed entirely of gold could undergo a slight alteration in shape without the gold in it altering at all;[16] but if the gold or other stuff of which the ring is entirely composed alters and is at all places where the ring is, throughout the alteration, then the ring itself has to alter. Let us, then, call anything that meets conditions (a) through (d) a physical very-near-body; and let us assume (because it makes things harder) that both a ring and the gold (stuff) in it are such very-near-bodies. Perhaps we can complete our definitional conditions of physical bodyhood, finally, by saying that:

(e) of necessity anything $x$ is a physical body *if and only if* $x$ is a physical very-near-body that is not essentially: such that any other physical very-near-body that is located wherever, but only where,[17] $x$ is located between any two times $t$ and $t'$ alters between $t$ and $t'$ if $x$ alters between $t$ and $t'$ (if there are no two physical very-near-bodies that could, at some time, exactly resemble one another, located wherever, but only where, $x$ is from $t$ to $t'$).[18]

Physical bodies like rings meet (e), because any gold ring can alter without its gold altering, even though that gold remains wherever and only where the ring is (remains the sole stuff of which the ring is composed) during the alteration. But the gold

[16] The sugar in sugar cane $a$ may be exactly like the sugar in sugar cane $b$, even though $a$ and $b$ are of different sizes and/or shapes, and thus not entirely alike. Shape and size are not relevant to what stuff is like the way they are relevant to what things made of stuff are like. And this key difference between 'stuff' and 'body' concepts we are building into our definition of physical bodyhood via condition (e).

[17] The qualification about sameness of location is to rule out problems that arise if we imagine physical bodies composed of different stuff at different times.

[18] The clause in parentheses is added to rule out Davidson's 'science fiction' cases where, e.g., two rings are located in the very same places. In such a case, the gold in one ring might alter without the other ring or its gold altering at all. See Davidson, 'The Individuation of Events', in *Essays in Honor of Carl G. Hempel*, ed., Rescher, Dordrecht: Reidel, 1969, p. 230f.

(or other stuff) in a given ring or other physical body does not meet condition (e), since, for example, any alteration in the gold of which a ring is composed that occurs while the gold remains the sole stuff of which the ring is composed necessitates an alteration in the ring itself.

We have, then, supplied conditions in terms of which one can define physical bodyhood in a way that does not seem *ad hoc* or arbitrary. Physical or material 'objects' like rings are not, however, the only entities that meet the definitional conditions we have offered.[19] Bodies of water are also physical bodies, and so too are bodies of air and other gaseous bodies. All such entities, I think, meet our conditions (a) through (e).[20] Given all the above, therefore, we can say that:

*⌜*a* is a physical body⌝ means about the same as ⌜there is a physical very-near-body *x* identical with *a* that is not essentially: such that any other physical very-near-body that is located wherever, but only where, *x* is located between any two times *t* and *t'* alters between *t* and *t'* if *x* alters between *t* and *t'* (if there are no two physical very-near-bodies that could, at some time, exactly resemble one another, located wherever, but only where, *x* is from *t* to *t'*)⌝.

And this definition by essence and accident involves only our primitives and notions definable via our primitives in ways we have indicated.

[19] Sums of physical bodies, etc., are, I assume, four-dimensional (possibly scattered) worms that are ruled out by condition (b). Our definition may not eliminate loosely organized or scattered 'bodies' from counting as bodies. However, piles of stones may in fact count as loosely organized *bodies* and not need to be eliminated. And if there exist such entities as scattered 'bodies' that are not really bodies, then perhaps our definition of physical bodyhood can be supplemented with certain spatial conditions, in order to eliminate them.

[20] I assume that gaseous or liquid bodies can alter with respect to the stuff of which they are composed, and even come to be made of solid stuff, via orderly processes. After all, it is natural to talk of the Earth as *it* was when *it* was in a gaseous state.

# 8. Reduction to Three Primitives

We have thus far been making use of five primitive (undefined) notion-clusters, in order to define some of the most metaphysically important concepts that philosophers have traditionally sought to understand or to define.[1] In the present chapter, I hope to make it plausible to think that we can reduce to three the number of primitive clusters of concepts required for definition by essence and accident of the various notions we have attempted to define in that manner. In particular, I shall argue that we may well be able to get along without the notions of an experience and of exact likeness as undefined concepts.

## I

What may enable us to eliminate the notion of an experience as a primitive without giving up our ability to define various concepts is the fact that certain highly distinctive ontological facts about experiences can be specified via the three notion-clusters we wish ultimately to retain as primitive, i.e., in terms

[1] The observant reader may by now have noticed that our group of primitive concepts closely parallels the group of basic concepts used by Hume in undertaking the metaphysical analyses and epistemological arguments of the *Treatise of Human Nature*. Hume uses such notions as resemblance and contrariety (close to our exact likeness); relation(s) in Space and Time; identity; and perception–impression and idea (which is close to our notion of an experience). Of course, there are also various differences between Hume's fundamental concepts and those used as fundamental in the present book (up till the present chapter).

of modal notions (*de re*), logical notions, and spatio-temporal notions.

Of necessity anything $x$ is an experience only if (a) $x$ is not temporally bound (and is thus contingent); (b) $x$ can be in at most one place (at only one point) at a time (and is thus essentially non-three-dimensional and non-voluminous); and (c) $x$ can be at different places at different times, if $x$ can have particular spatial location at all.[2]

These conditions eliminate bodies and selves (beings), which can take up volume and so can be located in more than one place at a given time. Times and places are clearly eliminated by (a) and (c) respectively. And natural necessities are ruled out by condition (a)—and probably by condition (b) as well. Various duos, trios, classes, species, etc., can also be seen to fail one or more of the above conditions of being an experience, if the reader takes the time to examine the matter.

What are not eliminated by these conditions are physical (non-Leibnizian) monads, and also, possibly, points on the surfaces of objects—conceived as other than points in Space, and so as capable of motion. And it is not easy to see how to distinguish monads from experiences via our three ultimate primitive notion-clusters. Experiences depend, essentially, on selves; and selves are essentially finite or essentially infinite in the past. However, monads essentially are such as to depend logically on classes of monads such that those classes are either essentially finite or essentially infinite in the past. Thus monad $a$ essentially depends on the class of entities identical with monad $a$ or monad $b$ (or, if one prefers, on the state of affairs monad $a$ or monad $b$ existing), which, in turn, is essentially finite or essentially infinite in the past.

[2] Cf. P. Ricoeur, *Husserl: An Analysis of his Phenomenology*, Evanston: Northwestern University Press, 1967, p. 47, where it is pointed out that according to Husserl, the psyche is located or localized, but not three-dimensional, or thus voluminous.

Notice, however, that for any given experience $e$, there could be infinitely many other experiences just like $e$ all of which were dependent on something (a self) that was not temporally bound and that was essentially finite in the past. Even if $e$ depends on a self that is essentially infinite in the past, it may be possible for there to be infinitely many experiences that are, at various times, exactly like $e$, as it is at those times, and that all logically depend on (are had by) some self that is essentially finite in the past. For such a self may exist forever in the future; and in that infinite time such a self could at fixed intervals have infinitely many different experiences each (at some time when it existed) exactly like $e$ (at that time).[3] A given monad $a$, on the other hand, can depend on the class of (entities identical with) monad $a$ or monad $b$; but it is not possible for infinitely many entities (monads) just like $a$ to depend on that class. And if it is possible for infinitely many entities (monads) just like $a$ to depend on the class of $b$ or $c$ or $d$, etc.—where such a class can be thought of as (simply) containing an infinity of entities (monads) that are essentially finite in the past and that are exactly like $a$ (at various times)—still (I am inclined to think) that class cannot itself be essentially finite in the past. After all, it is clearly possible for there to be a class, containing *infinitely many* entities that are essentially finite in the past and no other members, that is itself infinite in the past.

Given these facts, therefore, I think we are in a position to state a condition of experiencehood that rules out monads, as follows:

of necessity anything $x$ is an experience only if (d) it is possible for there to be infinitely many entities that are at various times exactly like $x$ as it is at those times, all of which

---

[3] We can surely imagine $e$ somehow lasting forever, while another person has infinitely many experiences (non-identical because brought into being in appropriately different ways, for example) each exactly like $e$ at some moment when $e$ exists.

depend on a single particular entity $y$ that is essentially finite in some temporal direction,[4] and not temporally bound.

Of course this definitory condition of experiencehood makes use of the notion of exact likeness, so we cannot claim yet to have shown how to eliminate the notion of experience in favour of the three ultimate primitives on which I hope to rely exclusively in giving definitions by essence and accident. Inasmuch, however, as we are later able to eliminate the notion of exact likeness in favour solely of our three ultimate primitives, we have here taken a major step in showing how the notion of experience can be eliminated as a primitive from our system of definitions. Notice too that in condition (d) we speak of 'infinitely many entities'. This is not in any obvious way a purely spatio-temporal notion; and it might be thought that we can eliminate the notion of experience as a primitive only by introducing some other new sort of primitive notion into our definitions. But this is not so; for instead of talking about infinitely many entities dependent on some different entity, we could talk about an (infinite) stretch of time after some given time $t$, and about all the times that exist or could exist at five minute intervals, or at some other interval, from $t$, and claim that at every one of those times there (tenselessly) exists a different entity like $x$. This would convey the idea of infinitely many entities without use of anything but clearly spatio-temporal notions, or other of the notions we wish ultimately to rely on or eliminate.

Our conditions (a) through (d) eliminate monads, but we have not yet shown how to eliminate points on the surfaces of

---

[4] I say 'in some temporal direction', rather than the perfectly accurate 'in the past', in order to avoid circularity in our ultimate system of definitions based on three primitives. For we have used the notion of 'self' in defining 'past' and the notion of 'experience' in defining 'self', so we should not use the notion of 'past' in defining 'experience'. Whether we can get by here with using 'in some temporal direction' instead of 'in the past' is not entirely clear to me.

physical objects, which seem to meet all these conditions. But this can be done quite easily. Points on, or in, bodies depend for their existence on the bodies on, or in, which they are points. We can, therefore, eliminate points on or in bodies by adding to our conditions of experiencehood that:

of necessity anything $x$ is an experience only if (e) $x$ does not depend on any (non-temporally-bound, contingent) essentially three-dimensional entity.

Even with condition (e), however, our conditions do not suffice to enable us to give an adequate definition of the notion of an experience. Certain psychical or mental dispositions, abilities or powers meet all the conditions we have laid down so far without themselves counting as experiences. My ability to think or my belief in human dignity or my psyche itself (whatever *that* is) may, for all we have said, be located in space (wherever I and my experiences are located), but such entities can no more be three-dimensional than experiences can be three-dimensional. And so on for our other conditions of experiencehood. Nor do I know how to distinguish between experiences and mental dispositions in terms of our three ultimate primitive concepts or concept-clusters. So I shall not claim that we have defined the notion of an experience, or that such a definition is possible by means of the ultimate primitives of our system of definitions. Fortunately, however, such definition is not clearly needed in order for us to be able to define all the concepts we want to in terms only of our three ultimate primitives. Even if we cannot define what it is to be an experience, we can define, via our ultimate primitives, a notion quite close to that of an experience: the notion for whose applicability conditions (a) through (e) are individually necessary and jointly sufficient, which is something like the notion of an experience *or* psychic disposition. And we can use this notion, instead of the notion of an experience, to define what it is to be a self (and thus to define the physical, physical body, etc.). This can be seen as follows.

Let us designate as an experience$_1$ anything meeting conditions (a) through (e) above. If we can later define the notion of likeness via our three ultimate primitives, the notion of an experience$_1$ can also be defined solely in terms of those primitives. And then our exiguously-based definition of selfhood, (conscious) beinghood, can proceed in a way nearly parallel to the way in which we framed our definition of selfhood in Chapter 4, with the notion of an experience$_1$ taking the place of the notion of an experience. Thus we can say that:

of necessity anything $x$ is a being only if (a) $x$ is mutable and contingent and it is possible for there to be an experience$_1$ that depends on $x$ and (b) $x$ does not depend on any experience$_1$.

We can call anything meeting (a) and (b) a cobrace$_1$. Some cobraces are not cobraces$_1$ and so are eliminated at this stage of our present attempt to define selfhood, or beinghood, though they were not eliminated at the parallel stage of our earlier definition of selfhood (or beinghood). My ability to have experiences, for example, is a cobrace, but not a cobrace$_1$, since that ability is an experience$_1$ and so depends on an experience$_1$. On the other hand, certain cobraces$_1$ are not cobraces, and these still require elimination, even though they were already eliminated at the parallel stage of our earlier definition of selfhood. For example, the class of experiences is not a cobrace, given our earlier definition of that term, but it is a cobrace$_1$, since it can be depended on by an experience$_1$ and does not depend on any given experience$_1$. Such entities, however, can be eliminated quite easily at the next stage of our definition of beinghood or selfhood. Just as we earlier defined the notion of an independent cobrace as a cobrace that does not essentially: exist only when another cobrace depends on it, we can now say that:

of necessity anything $x$ is a being only if (and an independent cobrace$_1$ if and only if) (c) $x$ is not essentially: depended on by *another* cobrace$_1$.

The class of experiences is no independent cobrace$_1$, since it essentially exists only if some more specific class of experiences—one such might be the class of visual experiences—depends on it. Similarly, the class of mental abilities and the class of visual experiences fail to meet condition (c) because they are of necessity depended on by more specific classes (or, if one wants, states of affairs).

We are still, however, left—at this stage of our present definition—with such more particular classes as the class of things identical with either experience $a$ or experience $b$. This class seems to meet (c), since even though it is essentially such as to be depended on by either $a$ or $b$, neither $a$ nor $b$ is a cobrace$_1$. At this point, however, we can add another condition, not parallel to any in our earlier definition of beinghood, to our present definition of that concept. We can say that:

of necessity anything $x$ is a being only if (d) $x$ can occupy a volume of space.

Condition (d) uses the spatial notion of volume, which we used (negatively) earlier to define what it is to be an experience$_1$. And (d) enables us to distinguish between beings, which can occupy volumes of space, and independent cobraces$_1$ like the class of (things identical with) experience $a$ or experience $b$, which cannot. Let us call any entity that is an independent cobrace$_1$ and that also meets (d) an independent cobrace$_2$.[5] The only kinds of

---

[5] One sort of entity our definition does not thus far enable us to eliminate is something like the class of experience $a$ or experience $b$ or physical body $c$. This class can occupy a volume of space and seems to meet conditions (a), (b), and (c) as well. But note this. Either beings essentially have psychic abilities or they do not. If they do, then we can add to our conditions of beinghood that anything $x$ is a being only if (d') $x$ is essentially: existent only when there are experiences$_1$. This condition (d') will eliminate the class of $a$ or $b$ or $c$, referred to just above. If, however, beings can exist

entities that seem to count as independent cobraces$_2$ are beings, and duos, trios, etc., of beings. And in that case we can complete our exiguously-based definition of beinghood much as we completed our definition of beinghood in Chapter 4 by saying that:

*⌜$a$ is a being(self)⌝ means approximately the same as ⌜there is an $x$ identical with $a$ such that $x$ is an independent cobrace$_2$ that depends on no other independent cobrace$_2$⌝.

The definition of selfhood just given in no way relies on the notion of experience as a primitive. It makes essential use only of the three ultimate primitives of our present enterprise, plus the notion of exact likeness, which we shall attempt to eliminate in favor of those three ultimate primitives in the next section of this chapter. Only then will it be possible for us to claim to have shown that the system of definitions by essence and accident in the present book can be made to rely on only three primitive notions or notion clusters.[6]

without any mental or psychic abilities, then we can say that of necessity anything $x$ is a being only if (d″) $x$ need not be depended on either by an experience$_1$ or by something voluminous. Condition (d″) eliminates the class of $a$ or $b$ or $c$, which, of necessity, is depended on either by an experience$_1$ ($a$ or $b$) or by a voluminous entity (body $c$). So whatever our final decision about whether beings need to have abilities, our definition (avoiding the notion experience) of beinghood can be supplemented in such a way as to handle the problem case of the class of $a$ or $b$ or $c$, and similar problem cases as well. And if we add (d′) or (d″) to our definitional conditions of the notion of an independent cobrace$_2$, then the final exiguously-based definition of beinghood offered in the text can remain verbally unaltered.

[6] In speaking here of a 'system of definitions', I do not mean to say that the totality of concepts defined by essence and accident necessarily constitutes some sort of natural class. However, all the concepts defined are metaphysically important concepts involved in most of our ordinary concepts and so central to our whole conceptual scheme; and each concept defined is involved in the definition of other concepts we define or requires for its own definition some of the other concepts we define (or both).

## II

There are two ways to eliminate a notion as primitive in a system of definitions. One is to show that the notion is not needed for the framing of the definitions of the system; and we have attempted to do just this with the notion of an experience in the previous section of this chapter. The other way to eliminate a notion as a primitive in a system of definitions is to show how it can be defined in terms of the other primitive notions of the system. And this is precisely what I should like now to do with the notion of exact likeness (or exact similarity).

Our definitions of exact similarity or likeness will occur in two parts. For we want to define both the idea of one thing $x$ (not) being exactly like or similar to another thing $y$ at a time $t$, and the idea of a given thing $x$ at a time $t$ (not) being exactly like or similar to the same thing $x$ at some other time $t'$, the idea of $x$ (not) altering. Both such types of talk about exact similarity or likeness were made use of by us in definitions by essence and accident, and both need to be defined away before we can get along without the notion of exact likeness or similarity as a primitive. One might, indeed, think at first that our defining away of similarity-notions need not be complex, need not occur in two distinct stages, since if one can construct a definition of the notion of a given thing at one time being exactly as it is at another, the definition of what it is for two things to be exactly alike at a time can be derived as a corollary in very simple fashion. But this is to assume that there is some easy and obvious way to translate talk about a thing not altering over time into talk about two things being exactly alike, or vice versa; and this assumption is in fact less warranted than it might at first seem. For example, we clearly cannot define ⌜$a$ altered between $t$ and $t'$⌝ by ⌜there is an $x$ that at some time is exactly like $a$ at $t$ and there is another thing $y$ that at some time is exactly like $a$ at $t'$ such that $x$ and $y$ are unlike at those two times⌝, since something can alter without there ever being anything like it. And a counterfactual analysis would fail for other reasons, aside from bringing in new primitive notions at a point where we wish to cut back on primitives. And surely, too, defining ⌜a and b are not exactly alike⌝ by ⌜there is an x identical with a and a y identical with b such that one of x and y has to alter in order for x and y to be exactly alike⌝ fails in its feeble attempt to define the notion of exact similarity between two things in terms of the notion of a single thing's altering, since the former notion reappears in the *definiens*.

What I should like to do now is to show how the notion of a single thing's (not) altering can be defined in terms of our three ultimate primitives, and then show how it is possible (in a rather complex way) to define the notion of two things' (not) being exactly alike in terms of the notion of a single thing's (not) altering. (The appearance of) successful completion of these two tasks will enable us (at least tentatively) altogether to eliminate the notion of exact similarity and the notion of an experience from among our primitives.

The basic idea behind the definition of alteration I shall propose is this. When an object alters, this involves certain states of affairs, etc., with certain ontological properties discussed earlier, 'doing' certain things; and these states of affairs and what they 'do' can, I think, be described fully by means solely of our three ultimate primitives. If an entity alters over time, is at one time not exactly as it is at another, incompatible or contrary states of affairs[7] obtain, each of which depends on the object or entity that alters. Thus if table a alters from red to green, there are at different times two states of affairs, a's being red and a's being green, that are incompatible and that are both dependent on a. Given, further, that the two states of affairs thus involved in alteration are not temporally bound, we can begin our definition of alteration by saying that:

[7] X and y are incompatible just in case it is impossible for x and y to exist at the same time.

of necessity anything $x$ alters between two times $t$ and $t'$ ($x$ at $t$ is unlike $x$ at $t'$) only if (a) there are a $y$ at $t$ and a $z$ at $t'$ that are incompatible and both dependent on $x$[8] and (b) $y$ and $z$ are both not temporally bound.[9]

Unfortunately, these conditions are insufficient to define alteration on the part of some entity $x$. For these conditions can be met by an entity without its altering. If I am ten miles from the Earth at one time and not at another, for example, I need not have altered between those two times, but there will be two temporally unbound states of affairs existing at two different times that are both dependent on me and incompatible with one another, namely, my being ten miles from the Earth and my failing to be ten miles from the Earth. It turns out that changes of position, i.e., motion or movement, on the part of an entity can cause it to fulfil conditions (a) and (b) without actually altering. But motion is a spatio-temporal notion, and since we are allowing ourselves such notions among our ultimate primitives, perhaps we can rule out such cases via our ultimate primitives and thereby come closer to our intended definition of alteration. Notice that alteration in a given thing is *independent* of where the thing is, whereas motion of a thing precisely is not. So we might try adding to our definition of alteration that:

(c) for all places $p$ and times $t''''$, $x$, $y$ and $z$ can each exist at $p$ and at $t''''$ and $y$ and $z$ can exist even if $x$ never moves.[10]

(There is no need to worry about coming or going out of existence on the part of $x$, since one of the states of affairs that involves, $x$'s not existing, does not depend on $x$.)

[8] It follows that $x$ does not depend on $y$ or on $z$.

[9] Variables in (b), and in later conditions, are bound by quantifiers in (a), as well as by the universal quantifiers preceding the whole statement.

[10] I assume that even entities essentially finite in the past can exist as early as we please. We can always imagine a speeding up of the processes and events in the universe as a result of which something $x$, which in fact occurs or exists only after $t$, occurs or exists long before $t$.

Another case that seems to present difficulties for the conditions we have suggested thus far is that in which a given thing $x$ is at one time near Mars and at another time not, just because Mars has in the meanwhile ceased to exist, and not because $x$ has altered, or moved, in any way in the process. This case, I think, cannot be ruled out as a case of alteration by the conditions proposed thus far, but it can, it seems, be ruled out if we add to our conditions of alteration that:

(d) neither $y$ nor $z$ depends on anything $c$ such that of necessity if one of $y$ or $z$ exists at some $t''$ and the other at some other $t'''$ and $c$ exists at both $t''$ and $t'''$, then either $x$ or $c$ is somewhere at $t'''$ where it is not at $t''$.

$X$'s being near Mars does depend on something $c$, namely, Mars, such that of necessity if one of $x$'s being near Mars or $x$'s not being near Mars exists at some $t''$ and the other at some $t'''$ and $c$ exists at both times, then either $x$ or $c$ is somewhere at $t'''$ where it is not at $t''$. On the other hand, neither $x$'s redness nor $x$'s greenness (or $x$'s non-redness) depends on anything in this way. $X$'s redness does depend on the species red thing, for example, but it is still not necessarily true that if $x$'s redness exists at $t''$ and $x$'s greenness at (another) $t'''$ and the species red thing at both times, then either $x$ or the species *red* thing will be somewhere at $t'''$ where it is not at $t''$. (At most it will be necessary only that $x$ or the species green thing be somewhere at $t'''$ where it is not at $t''$, in the specific case described.)

Our complex conditions (a) through (d) are, as far as I can tell, both individually necessary and jointly sufficient for alteration on the part of any $x$ between any $t$ and $t'$.[11]

[11] As we use 'alters between', something alters between $t$ and $t'$ only if it is at $t'$ not exactly as it is at $t$. In another sense, however, something can alter (in the interval) between $t$ and $t'$ even if it is at $t'$ exactly as it is at $t$, as long as there are two times $t''$ and $t'''$ either identical with $t$ or $t'$ or in between $t$ and $t'$ such that the thing in question is not at $t'''$ exactly as it is at $t''$. In cases of cyclical alteration, for example, something may alter between two given times in the second sense but not in the first.

*⌜$a$ alters between $t_0$ and $t_1$⌝ means about the same as ⌜there
are an $x$ identical with $a$, a $t$ identical with $t_0$, and a $t'$ identical
with $t_1$ such that there are a $y$ at $t$ and a $z$ at $t'$ that are incompatible and both dependent on $x$; $y$ and $z$ are both not
temporally bound; for all places $p$ and times $t''''$, $x$, $y$, and $z$
can each exist at $p$ and at $t''''$ and $y$ and $z$ can exist even if $x$
never moves; and neither $y$ nor $z$ depends on anything $c$ such
that of necessity if one of $y$ or $z$ exists at some $t''$ and the other
at some other $t'''$ and $c$ exists at both $t''$ and $t'''$ then either $x$
or $c$ is somewhere at $t'''$ where it is not at $t''$⌝.[12]

Let us now proceed to the definition of what it is for two
things to be (to some degree) unlike at a given time in terms of
our ultimate primitives plus the notion of something altering
between two times. Actually, I shall for heuristic reasons
attempt to define the notion of two things' being exactly alike—
the notion of dissimilarity or unlikeness (to some degree) at a
time then being definable by negation of our conditions for
exact likeness at a time. The reason for dealing primarily with
the notion of exact likeness is that one feels that it is very hard
for two things to be exactly alike at some time, but quite easy
for them not to be exactly alike at some time. So when and if
two things are exactly alike, there is, presumably, a very rare
or unexpected state of affairs in existence that involves both of
them, a state of affairs, moreover, such that it can continue to
exist, if either or both of the things *alter*, only if that altering
meets certain very specific and hard-to-achieve (or rarely-met-
with) conditions. And perhaps we can define what it is for *two
things to be exactly alike*, therefore, in terms of the strict
limitations that exist on how *they can alter* while (at the same
time) the state of affairs consisting in their being exactly alike
still exists, etc. These thoughts are not really arguments; but
they express why one might feel that for heuristic purposes, one
should first define exact likeness, rather than the absence of

[12] In this chapter, the values of the variables '$t_0$' and '$t_1$' are referring
temporal expressions.

exact likeness, in terms of the notion of a single entity's altering.

Perhaps, then, we can begin our definition of exact likeness by saying that:

> of necessity any two mutable and temporally unbound entities $x$ and $y$ are exactly alike at some $t$ only if (a) there exists at $t$ a temporally unbound entity $z$ dependent on mutable temporally unbound $x$ and on mutable temporally unbound $y$ (that is not identical with $x$) but not depended on by either $x$ or $y$.[13]

This condition is clearly not sufficient for exact likeness between appropriate $x$ and $y$, since in cases where $x$ and $y$ are not exactly alike there will be a $z$, e.g., $x$ and $y$'s *not* being exactly alike, that meets the above conditions. (Of course, when $x$ and $y$ are exactly alike, there will be a $z$ meeting condition (a), namely, $x$ and $y$'s being exactly alike, so (a) at least states a necessary condition of two appropriate things' being exactly alike.)

[13] I am only defining exact likeness between mutable unbound entities, because I do not know how to define exact likeness between immutable or bound entities. If so, then in order to complete our earlier definitions of 'is an alteration', 'is a motion', etc., *without using exact likeness as a primitive*, those definitions must be somewhat altered. Bound entities cannot be motions, etc., and we need not worry about exact likeness between such entities. But in order to rule out immutable entities such as various states of essentially-finite-in-the-past physical bodies from counting as motions on our definition of motion, while relying on only three ultimate primitives, we must understand the second part of our earlier definition of being a motion (see pp. 33, 105) as having to do only with mutable unbound entities. Then, in order to eliminate various states of things from counting as motions, we must add to that earlier definition something like: 'and if $x$ is immutable, $x$ essentially: exists at any $t''$ only if for every $t'''$ before and $t''''$ after $t''$, something moves in the interval between $t'''$ and $t''''$.' This will make immutable instant motions count as motions without making various states of things count as motions. Once our earlier definitions of motion, etc., have been adjusted in this kind of way, our elimination of exact likeness as a primitive can proceed in the way we are outlining here.

Note, however, the following important fact about exact alikeness. If $x$ and $y$ are exactly alike (mutable, etc., entities) at all times when they exist, then it cannot be the case that $x$ alters between two times $t$ and $t'$, $y$ never alters, and $y$ and $x$ exist at all the same times. So we can add to our definition that:

(b) $z$ cannot exist at all times when either $x$ or $y$ exists if $x$ alters between some two times and $y$ does not (or vice versa).

Condition (b) rules out many states of affairs that could obtain between $x$ and $y$ from counting as $z$'s meeting the conditions it, in conjunction with (a), sets. It rules out $x$ and $y$'s differing in colour, or $x$ and $y$'s not being exactly alike, since each of those states of affairs can exist at all times when $x$ or $y$ exists, even if $x$ alters and $y$ never does (or vice versa). Even $x$ and $y$'s being of exactly the same colour, or shade of red, does not meet the conditions set upon $z$ in condition (b), since two things may always be of exactly the same colour (or shade of red) and the one may alter with respect to something other than colour, while the other coexists but never alters.

There is, unfortunately, at least one state of affairs that (b) does not eliminate, namely, $x$ and $y$'s both not altering (remaining as they originally were). For this state of affairs can exist whenever $x$ or $y$ exists, only if it is not the case that $x$ alters and $y$ never does (or vice versa). If so, then (a) and (b) are not sufficient for $x$ and $y$'s being exactly alike, since they can be met if $x$ and $y$ never alter and are never exactly alike. Similarly, (b) does not rule out the case where $x$ and $y$ are always altering, and where there exists the state of affairs, $x$ and $y$'s both altering (undergoing alteration), which cannot exist at all times when $x$ or $y$ exists if $x$ alters and $y$ never does, or vice versa. But note that $x$ and $y$'s being exactly alike can exist even if neither is altering and even if both are altering. And the states of affairs mentioned just above can meet only one or the other of these two conditions. So perhaps we can rule out such problem cases by saying that:

(c) $z$ can exist at some time, or during some period, even if both $x$ and $y$ are altering at that time, or during that period, and even if both $x$ and $y$ are not altering at that time, or during that period.[14]

This does not yet rule out the case where $x$ and $y$ are always *either* both altering *or* both not altering, but that can easily be accomplished, I think, by adding a condition to the effect that:

(d) $z$ can exist between some $t'$ and $t''$ only if for every two times $t'''$ and $t''''$ between $t'$ and $t''$ or identical with $t'$ or $t''$, it is not the case that $x$ at $t''''$ is (to some degree) unlike $x$ at $t'''$ but $y$ at $t''''$ is not unlike $y$ at $t'''$.

Our conditions are not yet sufficient, however. The state of affairs consisting in $x$ and $y$'s being exactly alike except for their colour (and whatever else that involves) fails condition (b) since it can exist throughout the history of $x$ and $y$ even if $x$ alters (in colour) and $y$ never does, as long as $x$ never becomes exactly like $y$ in colour. But consider the state of affairs consisting of $x$ and $y$'s being exactly alike except for $x$'s being of the specific shade green$_n$ and $y$'s being of the specific shade red$_n$. The persistence of this state of affairs would be incompatible with $x$'s altering (in colour or otherwise) and $y$'s not altering at all, so it seems to meet condition (b); and, as far as I can tell, it meets all the other conditions proposed so far. To eliminate such states of affairs I (tentatively) propose the following further condition of exact similarity or likeness:

(e) $z$ does not depend on any temporally unbound immutable entity $w$ that depends on $x$ and $y$.

The problematic state of affairs just mentioned fails (e) because

---

[14] The notion of altering *at* a moment can be defined in terms of a nesting of intervals in which the moment occurs and altering between the beginning and end of such intervals, and thus in spatio-temporal terms.

it depends on the unbound but immutable state of affairs $x$'s being green$_n$ while $y$ is red$_n$, a state of affairs depending on both $x$ and $y$. However, it seems to me that $x$ and $y$'s being exactly alike does not fail (e), (in part) because that state of affairs does not depend on any immutable aspect of $x$ and $y$, can exist no matter how $x$ and $y$ are altering, as long as they alter together.

It has been pointed out to me by Harold Levin, however, that even these conditions are insufficient, through failing to rule out the case where $x$ and $y$ are 'incongruous counterparts', left hand/right hand 'mirror images' of one another that are not exactly alike or similar. But note two things. Such cases can be eliminated by adding to our definition that:

(f) $x$ and $y$ are not incongruous (incongruent), at $t$,

since the notion of incongruence is, presumably, a spatial notion. And, in addition, it is not necessary to eliminate such cases in order to complete our definitions by essence and accident in terms of three primitive concept-clusters. For conditions (a) through (e) seem to suffice to define the notion of two things' being exactly similar *or* exact incongruent counterparts. And I believe that that notion can, in fact, replace the notion of exact similarity between two things in all our earlier definitions, without affecting the accuracy of those definitions.

As far as I can tell, conditions (a) through (f) are necessary and sufficient for it to be the case that some mutable, etc., $x$ and $y$ are exactly alike at some time,[15] necessary and sufficient, indeed, by virtue of the very notion of exact likeness.

*⌜$a$ and $b$ are non-identical mutable unbound entities exactly alike at $t_0$⌝ means about the same as ⌜there are an $x$ identical with $a$, a $y$ identical with $b$, and a $t$ identical with $t_0$ such that $x$ and $y$ are non-identical mutable unbound entities and there is at $t$ a temporally unbound $z$ dependent on $x$ and $y$ but not

[15] I.e., for one thing, the only $z$'s meeting (a) through (f) are states of affairs involving $x$'s being exactly like $y$.

depended on by either $x$ or $y$; $z$ cannot exist at all times when either $x$ or $y$ exists if $x$ alters between some two times and $y$ does not (or vice versa); $z$ can exist at some time, or during some period, even if both $x$ and $y$ are altering at that time, or during that period, and even if both $x$ and $y$ are not altering at that time, or during that period; $z$ can exist between some $t'$ and $t''$ only if for every two times $t'''$ and $t''''$ between $t'$ and $t''$ or identical with $t'$ or $t''$, it is not the case that $x$ at $t''''$ is (to some degree) unlike $x$ at $t'''$ but $y$ at $t''''$ is not (to any degree) unlike $y$ at $t'''$; $z$ does not depend on any temporally unbound immutable entity $w$ that depends on $x$ and $y$; and at $t$, $x$ and $y$ are not incongruent or incongruous[7].

I hope we have made good our promise to define exact likeness or similarity between two entities at a given time in terms of the notion of altering, or alteration, by single entities over time, and have also shown how one can in general define the notion of (exact) similarity or likeness, as used by us here, in terms of our three ultimate primitives. Inasmuch as we earlier showed how we can get along without the notion of an experience in framing our definitions by essence and accident, the upshot of our argument in this chapter is that all the various definitions by essence and accident of the present book may well be able to be formulated solely in terms of the three clusters of primitives that I said I wished ultimately to rely on.

The definitions we just gave of exact similarity or likeness at a time and of alteration over time have one possible drawback. Those definitions operate on the assumption that when things alter or are exactly alike, certain states of affairs that can be very precisely pinpointed via our primitives exist and/or cease to exist. So our definitions, taken together with plausible other assumptions about the world, involve us in an ontological commitment to (certain sorts of) states of affairs.[16] But this is just another case where ideology contracts at the expense of

[16] But the *notion* of a state of affairs is not used in those definitions, for this would involve a new primitive.

expanded ontology. If we want a definition (and elimination from primitive status) of the notions of alteration and exact likeness, such expanded ontology (and whatever implausibility accrues to the assumption that there are such entities as states of affairs) seems to be the price we have to pay. At least it is good to have the *choice* between limiting one's ontology and limiting one's ideology.

Our efforts in this book have attempted to serve two different goals of metaphysics. In metaphysics one often seeks definitions of important concepts like those we have attempted to define; but one also is often interested in understanding and stating some of the more important (*de re*) ontological relations between entities of various kinds. One wants to know, for example, how psychic entities are related to physical ones, how beings are related to their experiences, how things are related to the alterations that take place in what they are like, etc. And we have in this book also been answering these kinds of questions about the ontological relations between entities. The reason why we have been able to do both these things in the present work is simple. Definition by essence and accident requires the specification of ontological relations of exact similarity, necessary coexistence, logical incompatibility, and logical dependence between various kinds of entities, and in particular between entities falling under concepts being defined by essence and accident and other entities. I hope, then, that our definitions of key categorial concepts also serve to deepen our understanding of the (*de re*) ontological relations among the various kinds of entities there are or (epistemically) may be in the universe.

The analytic definitions by essence and accident offered here are, some of them, highly complex, because I have attempted to state conditions that exclude all counterexamples, however wild, that could not, in good conscience, be ruled out a priori as logically impossible. Many of these definitions could be mistaken. There are probably counterexamples I have not considered that can cause trouble for some of the claims and definitions of this book. However, since definition by essence and accident via our three ultimate primitives, or at least via our five original primitives, seems in so many cases to offer at least somewhat plausible analyses of basic concepts that have not been successfully analysed in any *other* way, this will perhaps encourage those who do find counterexamples to some of our definitions to seek for ways to reformulate or add to those definitions via our primitives that avoid those counterexamples. I think one must, in other words, distinguish our general enterprise and techniques from the particular, and no doubt partial, realization of them that we have managed here. In attempting to define the concepts analysed in this book, I have myself taken many false steps that had to be corrected in the light of various counterexamples. And the definitions finally arrived at are only those to which I *at this moment* know of no counterexamples. But philosophy of the kind done in the present work is intended as the beginning, not the final resting place, of a cooperative enterprise. And I can only hope that those who approach this work critically will also approach it in that spirit.

# Appendix: Propositions and Properties

In Chapter 6, we discussed the nature and existence conditions of facts (if they exist) and claimed that (by definition) every fact is the truth (being true) of some proposition. And the theory of facts presented in Chapter 6 clearly does provide ontological clarification about (the category of) facts, if it is true or even just on the right track. Many philosophers, however, have been perplexed about the nature or existence of propositions; since on our theory a fact is the truth of a proposition, our theory about the nature of facts probably would not be complete unless we were *already* clear about the nature of propositions or could *provide* some sort of plausible theory about the nature of propositions (if they exist). Since I am not very happy with the views about propositions with which I am acquainted, I would like, for the sake of completeness, to outline a view of the nature of propositions. I shall then attempt briefly to say what I think (platonic) properties or universals are (if they exist), and to show that knowledge about the nature of properties or universals is as useful in clarifying the nature of temporally unbound states of affairs as is knowledge of the nature of propositions in helping us understand temporally bound facts.

## I

When philosophers speak of propositions, they mean to refer to something that (in most cases) exists and is true or false independently of being encapsulated or conventionally expressed in words, to some sort of necessarily existent platonic entity with a truth value. Consider the state of affairs: its being logically possible that something is red at $t$ (where 't' is a constant referring, say, to the present moment). Just as Helen's being beautiful lasts precisely as long as Helen is beautiful, so too, presumably, its being (logically) possible that something is red at $t$ is a state of affairs that exists (if at all) just in case it is (logically) possible that something is red at $t$. The latter state of affairs, furthermore, can also be (rigidly) designated by 'the (logical) possibility that something is red at $t$', just as we can substitute 'the beauty of Helen' for 'Helen's being beautiful' and preserve our reference. It would seem, in addition, that the logical possibility that something is (or should be or should have been) red at $t$ is a necessary existent (if it exists at all). For given our view in Chapter 5 that the $f$ness of $x$ essentially exists just if $x$ is $f$ (if the $f$ness of $x$ exists at all), we can, I think, infer that the logical possibility that something is red at $t$ essentially exists just in case it is logically possible that something is red at $t$ (if that possibility exists at all). And it is logically necessary for it to be logically possible that something is red at $t$.

I think that if it exists, this necessarily existent state of affairs, the logical possibility that something is red at $t$, is the proposition that something is red at $t$. And I also believe that all propositions can be identified with possibilities (or, as we shall see, with impossibilities) of this type. For one thing, possibilities of the kind just mentioned all seem to have the characteristics normally attributed to propositions. The logical possibility that something is red at $t$ exists (if at all) independently of human or other linguistic conventions or acts, indeed exists necessarily; and it is imperceptible and weightless, and thus presumably 'abstract', in the way propositions are supposed to be. Moreover, the possibility that something is red at $t$ is logically immutable, in the way that propositions are typically thought to be; for the possibility that something is red at $t$ can alter only if it can be logically possible *in different ways at different times* that something should be red at $t$. And nothing can be logically possible in different ways at different times.

At this point we have two options—assuming that we wish to take platonic entities seriously. We can say that there are states of affairs, possibilities and impossibilities, with many of the same properties propositions are supposed to have, but not identical with propositions. Or we can claim that those states of affairs are what propositions turn out to be. Certainly ontological simplification, Ockham's Razor, favours the latter move. Nor does the identification of propositions with certain logical possibilities (or impossibilities) seem to offend any of our prior clear intuitions about what propositions are like. But what probably most favours the identification of propositions with possibilities (or impossibilities) of the above sort is the way such identification helps us to understand how propositions can be necessary existents. One of the chief problems about propositions, for philosophers, has been their putative necessary existence; philosophers have been perplexed about how there could be such a thing as a necessarily existent proposition. The claim that possibilities of the sort we have mentioned exist by necessity seems much less perplexing and mysterious, on the face of it. For given what we said about states of affairs in Chapter 5, it should be clear why the possibility that something is (or should be or should have been) red at $t$ essentially: exists just in case it is possible that something is (or should be or should have been) red at $t$, and thus is a necessary existent, if it exists at all. Identification of this possibility with the proposition that something is red at $t$ thus helps us to explain how there can be such an entity as a necessarily existent proposition.[1]

In identifying various propositions with logical possibilities of

[1] I tend to assume that the logical possibilities we have mentioned, and propositions, exist at every time and place, of necessity. Most adherents of propositions have assumed that propositions were not in space or time, in great part, I think, because they thought that only thus could the necessity and immutability of propositions be explained. But our explanation of the necessity and immutability of propositions did *not* require the assumption that propositions are not in space or time—and I can think of no reason to make that assumption. It seems plausible, further, to think of possibilities as existing everywhere at all times, necessarily.

a certain kind, we are denying the traditional view that propositions are the meanings of sentences. But this latter view is
fraught with difficulties. It has a hard time dealing with such
putative ego-centric particular propositions as the proposition
that I exist and it cannot easily account for propositional truth,
since it is not easy to see how meanings can be true. What
further militates against the idea that propositions (as traditionally conceived) are sentence meanings is the questionableness of
the assumption that the meanings of words or sentences are
platonic entities that exist independently of linguistic conven-
tion(s) and usage. It has been argued by Dennis Stampe[2] that
the meaning of a sentence is not some (perhaps platonic) entity
that the sentence means, in great part on the basis of linguistic
evidence that indicates that 'means' (as applied to sentences) is
not a normal transitive verb. Stampe's own inclination is to
conclude that there are no such things as sentence meanings;
but I would like to suggest a view of what meanings are that
seems to me to have a good deal of plausibility and that avoids
saying that meanings are entities meant. It seems to me, rather,
that the (present) meaning of 'men exist' is perhaps just: the
phrase 'men exist' 's present way of meaning (being meaningful).
And perhaps the (present) meaning of the word 'red' is just:
'red' 's present way of meaning (being meaningful). What tends
to support this view about sentence and word meanings is an
interesting parallel with certain states of affairs we mentioned
earlier. Consider 'Helen's looks' (or 'Helen's appearance'). Such
a phrase results from nominalizing a sentence or phrase containing the verb 'looks' (or 'appears'). Furthermore, Helen's (present) looks is just Helen's present way of looking. In the light
of this example, it seems somewhat plausible to imagine that
'the (present) meaning of "men exist" ' is a nominalization that
derives from the verb 'to mean' and that the present meaning of
'men exist' is just the phrase 'men exist' 's present way of being
meaningful. On this view, meanings of words or sentences are

---

[2] 'Towards a Grammar of Meaning', *Phil. Review* 77, 1968, pp. 137–74.

perishable states of affairs that essentially: exist only when there are (contingently existing) linguistic conventions or usages in force. If so, the identification of propositions with sentence meanings would deprive propositions of their platonic status and of their traditionally conceived status as bearers of truth value independently of the existence of any linguistic (or other symbolic) conventions or usages. Since this would not allow propositions to fulfil one of the major purposes for which they were traditionally conceived, it would seem to be a mistake to identify propositions with meanings.

The real test of the theory of propositions we have proposed is whether it can account completely and coherently for propositional truth—allowing, in particular, for propositions to be true independently of (human) convention(s). The proposition that Helen is white at $t$ is, on our view, the logical possibility that Helen is white at $t$, or, perhaps, alternatively, the logical possibility of Helen's being white at $t$. That proposition is true just in case that possibility is realized; so it is natural to conclude that on our view the truth of a proposition is the realization of the logical possibility that it is, i.e., is the realization of that proposition. Such a consequence of our theory is certainly initially odd. Is it really possible that truth of a proposition is realization of that proposition and that truth of a proposition is truth of a logical possibility? Does it even make sense to speak of a logical possibility's being true or of a proposition's being realized? Let us examine these difficulties.

The most basic difficulty with the theory of propositional truth just suggested is its consequence that one and the same entity can be both true and realized. But this consequence is not as odd as it might at first seem. Someone's wishes (or dreams or worst fears) can come true; and they can also be fulfilled or realized. (Furthermore, the notion of a wish's coming true is closely related to the notion of truth as applied to propositions, but that is a story for another occasion.) Moreover, there are clear cases where we naturally speak of proposition-like entities, entities capable of being literally true or false, as being realized, or fulfilled. Thus, in speaking of certain geometrical claims, the mathematician E. T. Bell writes that in such and such cases 'the hypothesis of the acute angle is realized'.[3] Also it is perfectly idiomatic to speak of a prediction (that has come *true*) as having been realized, or fulfilled. But if some true proposition-like entities are or have been *realized*, then that is evidence for our view that propositions are possibilities (whose truth is their realization), since possibilities are, *par excellence*, those entities that are capable of being realized. So perhaps our theory of propositions and propositional truth is not, in the end, as strange as it might first appear to be.

Our theory, furthermore, has the advantage of explaining how there can be truth without convention, since it is clear that certain logical possibilities can be realized even if there are no conventions. But such truth without convention is in a way quite odd. It cannot be like the truth of an assertion (asserting)[4] or of a sentence, since the truth of an utterance or of a sentence like 'men exist' involves more than the mere realization of the logical possibility that men exist, and so is different from the 'bare bones' of truth involved in propositional truth. But if propositional truth (except for propositions about language) does not involve the truth of sentences or utterances governed by certain conventions and is independent of the existence of convention(s), then perhaps we can only make sense of propositional truth in terms of the notion of the realization of a certain kind of possibility. Perhaps the only kind of truth that can exist independently of conventions and assertions is a truth that involves *only* the realization of certain possibilities; so if we insist by dint of our talk about propositions, in talking about truth that is independent of linguistic convention, etc., perhaps all we can or should mean by the truth of a proposition is the

---

[3] *Men of Mathematics*, N.Y.: Simon and Schuster, 1965, p. 305.

[4] I shall not attempt to refute the view that assertings (or statings or believings) are not true or false, because acts, or events, and dispositions cannot be true or false; but I do think there are reasons for thinking such a view to be mistaken.

realization (being realized) of a certain kind of possibility.

This is especially true when one considers that one *cannot* in general explain propositional truth—where propositions are true independently of linguistic conventions—in terms of the sentences that would be true if they expressed certain propositions as a matter of linguistic convention or usage. One cannot, that is, say that a proposition that *p* counts as true just in case if any sentence were conventionally used to express precisely the proposition that *p*, it would bear relation *R* to reality— where *R* is whatever conventionally existing relation[5] it is that exists between true sentences (of the appropriate kind) and reality. For surely the claim or proposition that there are no conventions is itself only contingently false; yet the theory just suggested cannot account for the possibility of its truth, since in no possible circumstances could a sentence as a matter of usage or convention express that proposition and be true. The same sorts of problems exist in many other cases, and what these problems show is that one cannot *in general* analyse what it is for a proposition to be true in terms of the conventionally existing relation(s) to reality that would be had by any true sentences that expressed it. The failure of such attempts to analyse propositional truth while leaving it independent of the actual existence of linguistic conventions, etc., shows, I think, that propositional truth cannot be analysed, even hypothetically, in terms of linguistic conventions, i.e., shows that propositional truth is in no way a matter of linguistic convention;[6] and once one sees that this is so, it should be easier to see how propositional truth may *just* involve some totally *non-conventional*

---

[5] A conventionally existing relation only exists if certain conventions exist; sentences (can be used to) express truths only if there exist at least implicit linguistic conventions.

[6] Many philosophers who have seen that propositions were not linguistic entities (bound to any given language) have nonetheless failed to see that propositional *truth* cannot be conventional, exist by virtue of certain conventions. Among them is Austin. Cf. G. J. Warnock, 'A Problem about Truth' in G. Pitcher, ed., *Truth*, Englewood Cliffs: Prentice Hall, 1964, p. 67n.

relation or property like realization, as our own theory claims.[7]

I should stress finally that necessarily false propositions should, on our theory, be thought of as logical impossibilities; the logical impossibility (proposition) that I be (am) a prime number cannot be true, inasmuch as an impossibility cannot be realized. Necessary propositions, I think, are just logical possibilities that *have* to be realized.[8] Now that we have said something about propositions and their truth, I would like to suggest a parallel theory about properties (universals) and their instantiation or exemplification.

## II

I would like to propose, tentatively, that if the property, say, of redness (of being red) exists at all, it is just the logical possibility of being red. Other properties or universals can be

[7] What happens in the case where it is true that there are no conventions, but it is not the case that if there were conventions and a sentence that expressed the proposition that there are no conventions, that sentence would be true, is not like what happens in the cases that give rise to the semantic paradoxes. In the latter cases, the notion of truth breaks down; one does not know how to apply the notion without getting into contradictions. But in the counterexample case we mentioned, the case where there truly are no conventions, it is not as if the notion of truth breaks down or involves one in contradictions. Rather it is just the theory of truth we are criticizing that is clearly inadequate to explaining the truth of the proposition that there are no conventions in those situations in which it *is* true. And clearly, if we talk about propositions as true independently of conventions, we want to allow that and explain how the proposition that there are no conventions can be true in the absence of any conventions.

[8] I do not think we should identify necessarily true propositions with certain logical necessities *rather than* with certain logical possibilities that have to be realized, because if such logical necessities are not (also) (identical with) possibilities, it is hard to see how such things could be *realized*. Since we clearly have a motive to treat truth as realization wherever we can, we should identify necessary propositions with logical possibilities that have to be realized (and that *may*, as a result, be or constitute logical necessities as well).

identified with possibilities (or impossibilities) *of this kind* in a similar way. Most platonists (Platonists) have held that universals were necessarily existent, immutable, abstract, imperceptible, weightless entities; and in the light of what was said in the previous section, it should be clear that if such possibilities as the logical possibility of being red exist at all, they are necessarily existent, etc., and so are not, on the face of it, implausible candidates for identification with platonic universals, properties, attributes, qualities, or what have you. Moreover, given our identification, it is, I think, easier to understand how there can or might be such a thing as a necessarily existent, immutable, etc., universal.

On this theory, to possess (have) a property or universal is to realize a certain kind of logical possibility. The chair possesses redness just in case it realizes the logical possibility of being red, which is the property of redness. Similarly, redness is 'in' a chair when redness, a certain possibility, is realized by the chair. It has often been said that the whole notion of possession, having or participation in a property or universal—or of a universal's being in something—is metaphorical and/or mysterious.[9] The idea of realizing a possibility is probably also ultimately mysterious—even if not metaphorical. But, in any case, by identifying possession of a property, etc., with the realization of a certain sort of logical possibility, we have reduced two mysteries to one—and have, perhaps, gone from the metaphorical to the literal.[10] Inasmuch, furthermore, as we have also used the notion of realization to explain propositional truth, we have perhaps even reduced *three* mysteries to one. Of course, all this does not mean that truth is possession or

[9] Cf. F. M. Cornford, *From Religion to Philosophy*, N.Y.: Harper and Row, 1957, p. 255.

[10] The idea that a universal's being in things is just its being realized by things helps to solve or dissolve the old problem about how a universal can be in differently located things at the same time. If the sense of 'in' is not one of spatial location, and if being in just involves realization by, then there is no more problem about a universal's being in different things

participation or instantiation, or that propositions are properties. For realizable propositions are different logical possibilities from those logical possibilities that are universals or properties, and thus the realization (possession, instantiation) of a property will not generally be the realization (truth) of a proposition.

If propositions exist and what we have said about them is correct, then the fact that Helen is white at $t$, the truth of the proposition that Helen is white at $t$, is just the realization of the (logical) possibility that Helen is (should be or should have been) white at $t$. And I think there is similar reason to hold that if properties exist, unbound states of affairs are the realizations of those possibilities that are properties or universals. Helen's being white, for example, may well be identical with the realization of the logical possibility of being Helen and white, which, in turn, is just the being possessed (the instantiation or exemplification) of the property of being Helen and white. For one thing, if platonic universals exist, then Helen's being white and the realization of the logical possibility of being Helen and white (or the being possessed of the property of being Helen and white) will, *ex vi terminorum*, be mutually logically dependent temporally unbound entities, and surely that gives us reason to consider them identical. Similarly, there being ravens may be the realization of the logical possibility of being a raven (or the exemplification of the universal ravenhood). If platonic entities exist, then in some sense facts are aspects of (states of affairs involving) propositions, whereas temporally unbound states of affairs are aspects of (states of affairs involving) properties or universals. And the reason why facts cannot alter but some unbound states of affairs can may then be that propositions are possibilities with time built into them in such a way that they cannot be realized (true) in different ways at different times,

than there is about a possibility's being *realized by* different things (at the same time). For the same reason, the old question whether universals are *wholly* or *partly* in each thing that possesses them dissolves. For what sense, e.g., does it make to ask whether the logical possibility of being red is wholly or only partly realized by a given red thing?

whereas some properties are possibilities that *can* be realized (exemplified, etc.) in different ways at different times. The possibility that Helen be white at *t* cannot be realized in different ways at different times, so the fact that is its realization cannot alter. But the possibility of being Helen and white *can* be realized in different ways at different times (if Helen is different shades of white at different times), so the state of affairs, Helen's being white, that is its realization *can* alter over time. The difference between the kind of possibilities propositions are and the kind of possibilities properties are also enables us to explain why facts are temporally bound and certain other states of affairs are not, but there is no space to go into the details of this here. In any case, one thing temporally unbound states of affairs, facts, universals and propositions all have in common, on our present theory, is that they all *are* states of affairs, and obey the basic 'logic' for states of affairs outlined in Chapter 5.

# Index of Definitions

# General Index